GROWING WITH GAMES

Making Your Own Educational Games

Sally Goldberg

Ann Arbor   The University of Michigan Press

To Cynthia, Deborah, and my husband Paul.
Cynthia helped me develop the games.
Deborah helped me refine the games.
Paul helped me enjoy seeing the children grow.

Copyright © by the University of Michigan 1985
All rights reserved
Published in the United States of America by
The University of Michigan Press
Manufactured in the United States of America

1999   1998   1997   1996   4   3   2

Library of Congress Cataloging-in-Publication Data

Goldberg, Sally, 1947–
  Growing with games.

  Bibliography: p.
  1. Educational games. 2. Creative activities and
seat work. I. Title.
GVI480.G64   1985   649'.51   85-8541
ISBN 0-472-06364-2 (pbk.)

Acknowledgments

To Bea Alberelli, occupational therapist and teacher, who taught me many techniques for helping children. Thanks also to Marge Prenner, teacher, who took so much interest in using many of these methods. Special appreciation to Rose Goldberg, my aunt, who encouraged me through every step of the way.

Marilyn Finkelstein, director of the Parent Center, at Miami-Dade Community College, helped me set up my first location for working with children. Sylvia Sondak, director of Congregation Bet Breira Preschool, and Sandi Kramer, director of Temple Beth Am Preschool, gave me additional opportunities to develop my ideas. For all their support, I extend them special thanks.

To Nellie Justi who types so well, thank you for making this book possible. Tanya Rovin and Carolyn Glynn are my dedicated readers, and I continue to appreciate their time and effort.

Preface

When my second daughter was born in February, 1981, every-one asked, "Are you going to do the same educational activities with her that you did with your first daughter?" At that time the answer to that question was unknown. I did not know for sure what I would do until it came time to do it. As it turned out, I chose to do everything and more. She had the advantage of having the whole program all worked out as explained in my first book, *Teaching with Toys: Making Your Own Educational Toys*, so that we could with ease proceed with her guidance in an educationally positive way.

When my older daughter was three, I began collecting more and more information about valuable activities to do with her. I made lists, but the more I studied the longer my lists became. At that point I could see the activities began to center themselves around categories. Then I wrote out the games for each category on a separate sheet so that I could easily add new ideas. This new way enabled me to keep track of what I was doing with her. I then put each of the games on an index card and grouped them by category. By putting each game on a card and showing her a group of cards from which she could pick, she got the sense of beginning, ending, and accomplishing a set of activities. In addition, she had the fun of choosing what we were going to do together. The identifying category symbols became a learning experience itself. For example, one category of game we identified as the "?" games.

Now that my daughter is six years old, whenever we have free time together, she says, "Mom, let's do the games." The amount of time we work at it at a sitting varies. If we have fifteen minutes, we do only a few. With more time, we do more. It doesn't matter; the important part is that we both have direction in spending play time together in a satisfying and productive way.

Contents

List of Games

Introduction

While *Teaching with Toys: Making Your Own Educational Toys* is for the birth through preschool age group, this book is a guide for the preschool through first grade level of development. Because today's parents are involved in their children's education for many different reasons, these ideas are presented to make that involvement easier, more efficient, and enjoyable.

No matter what the situation of the child, it is helpful for parents to know what is considered a well-rounded supplementary educational program for their child. For a child with a learning disability, the games will help to counteract the difficulty; for an advanced child, they will provide enrichment; and for any child, they will foster continued developmental growth. All the games are designed to help a child to reach his full potential.

The games accomplish important objectives and can be tailored to the ability and personality of the child. The same game can be used repeatedly, but the child will get more out of it as he grows. They can also be used with two different children, each child doing the task in a different appropriate way. The repetition of the games is an important part of their effectiveness.

Most of the games are designed from available household items or no materials at all. They feature how to use what you already have in an educational way. There is also a section on the home environment as an educational center and parents as teachers. Children spend many hours in their home and with their parents. There are many educational activities that can easily be done almost any time and almost anywhere. The key to parent teaching is that it must be done through a games format. Most successful in-home teaching has a different style from that of a classroom.

For this age group the educational topics are reading, writing, language, listening and thinking, midline, game playing, mathematics, gross motor, and fine motor. These are foundation skills for later learning. They follow the prerequisite skills of self-awareness, colors, letters, numbers, shapes, and beginning reading as described in *Teaching with Toys*. Since parents may feel some of the games are more appropriate for their children than others, and since children will show preference too, there is flexibility in this kind of program. The idea is to turn many parent-child interactions into positive supportive experiences.

Each of the following chapters explains the games for one of the topics. At the end of the book are cards that can be cut out of the book that list each game on one side and a symbol that identifies the game on the other. When ready to play the games from one of the topics, all the cards from that topic should be laid out on a table, symbol side up, in front of the child and parent. Learning to recognize the symbol itself will be incidental learning. Once laid out, any kind of appropriate counting or mathematical activity can be played with the cards before the actual games are selected for play. Then the child may choose his own game, pick it up, and try to read it the best he can according to his own reading level. The parent can help with the reading as necessary. Selecting the game in this way adds an element of surprise to the activity. For some of the topics, one of the cards is a happy face instead of a game. If the child picks that card, he may pick again.

At this point parent and child begin the game. Together they can gather whatever materials they need and then begin to play. Some of the games are short and give the child and parent an immediate feeling of accomplishment. Others are

longer and give the feeling they have shared an in-depth play time together. Because parents will be aware of the objective behind a particular play activity, they will feel satisfied that they have spent play time with their child in an enriching way. In addition, because of the focus on variety, parents can feel relaxed that their children are getting exposure to a wide variety of important developmental play experiences.

When you finish all the games in one topic, you can lay out the cards for another. If you go through the topics in order, it will take quite a lot of time to get back to any topic again. This type of rotation will make all the games in a topic seem new and interesting to both parent and child. It will reduce both parent and child desire to keep buying new games.

If a child has either a weakness or an interest in one of the topics, you can use those games more frequently. It is not necessary for all children to go through all the games. If a child does not want to do a game one day he may want to come back to it another time. This approach is designed to meet the needs of an individual child and not to fit the child into a broad program. It can be as broad or as narrow as the people who use it prefer.

Another advantage to playing the games with easily accessible household items is that some of the games can be practiced at other times. For example, a game like the fine motor game of wringing out a washcloth can be done at bath time as well. Therefore, the formal games situation can be a reminder about activities to do during the child's daily routine.

All of the stimulation activities of today relate back to natural upbringing of yesteryear. In the old days when families lived closer together, grandparents, aunts, uncles, and cousins were around to take over child care of the very young. They talked to the children often, recited nursery rhymes, and read stories, all natural ways to develop language. Later as children grew and learned skills of the home and family work, they helped out with that work. Much of it helped to develop fine and gross motor skills as well as language, reading, mathematics, and reasoning. This whole process was educationally stimulating and naturally led to the development of productive individuals.

Movement for children of all ages is developmentally stimulating. For a baby, movement through space either on its mother's back or as part of daily walks in carriages and strollers is an important developmental activity. Other home physical work is also important to an older growing child. A playground is a paradise for children. It is a place with equipment designed for them to move in every direction.

Age-old games like hide-and-seek and catch serve a developmental purpose. In our fast paced and constantly changing world, many of the old games should be passed on. Some new ones are excellent, but they should enrich and not replace important basic activities for children.

Today we have a large population of learning disabled children. They have average or high IQs but have learning difficulties in some areas, such as reading, writing, mathematics, or all three. Many of the problems relate back to stimulation activities that were missing from the child's early experiences. The fault is not with the parents or home life but with our change to a technological, mechanized life-style.

In this book as well as in *Teaching with Toys*, I give ideas to parents to help them round out experiences for their children. I give hints on how they can fill in for some of the important activities that may be left out. Through basic activities, we can help children of all abilities, interests, and backgrounds.

1

Games for Reading Development

One of the most time-honored and enjoyable child care activities, passed on from generation to generation, is reading to your child. Reading is a natural part of our life-style and is something children should be aided in from the early years. Just as exposure to spoken words leads to speech, exposure to written words leads to reading.

Children learn to talk because people talk to them. In the same way they will learn to read if people read to them. Books with large print are especially helpful in the beginning because you can easily point to the words as you read them. Continue to point to the words you are reading in all books. This will connect for them the spoken word with its written form. The titles which are repeated on the first inside page are large and provide excellent reading practice. Games you make that require the children to follow directions written on cards are also beneficial.

The repetition of seeing words in different books and in different places will lead to the recognition of words. Because we have a culture filled with bright signs, those large words can be used for reading enrichment throughout the child's day. In addition, there are some simple exercises you can do with children to help them read and comprehend better.

Letter cards are a good way to learn the letters. You can write them on index cards, hole punch the corners, loop them with yarn, and make up your own games that will teach them names and then sounds. The sounds of the vowels, both short and long, will need the most repetition. Games with letters and their sounds combined will games with words and sentences will lead to successful reading.

BOOKSHELF BOOKS

Objective
To read to your child.

About the Game
At this stage of development, the child is probably competent in some beginning reading skills, but this is the parent's time to pick up some higher level books. You can choose books from a home or public library to introduce the child to thought-provoking situations that will help him grow in a social or educational way. Any book that a child responds to positively is appropriate because this is a time to share a quiet experience together. It will also serve to build receptive and expressive vocabulary for the child and the desire to improve his own reading level.

How to Play
Books on a child's bookshelf should be set up for rotation. When you pick the one, two, or three for your reading session, take them from one end and be sure to return them to the other. This will make all books seem new and interesting. Of course, if there is a favorite it is fine to read that again and again. Always try to introduce new books but do not force them on the child. That defeats the whole purpose of a positive reading experience.

The following is a list of books that I recommend for the early years. Most of them are available in your local library or bookstore. There are many more that are equally good, but these are ones that I know about and like very much.

Social

Families Live Together by Esther K. Meeks and Elizabeth Bagwell.

A compilation of beautiful full color photographs about families doing different activities and expressing different feelings. It has a nice introduction about animal families.

My House Photographs by Heinz Kleutmeier for Golden Press.

A short book with durable cardboard pages and one sentence per page. Each page is a photograph of a small child doing something around the house familiar to all children. Other books in the series include: *Pet Friends, Busy Bear, Here We Go, Listen to That, The Farm, The Seasons, Baby's Rainbow Pals, Baby Animals, Play School, Puppies,* and *Kittens.*

Children's Manners Book by Alida Allison.

An easy-to-read book with simple colorful illustrations about polite things to say in different situations.

How Do I Put It On? by Shigeo Watanabe.

A bear gets dressed all by himself, first the wrong way and then the right way. The illustrations and concepts are appealing, especially to young children who are learning to dress themselves. The print is large. Other books in the series include: *I Can Ride It, Get Set! Go!, What a Good Lunch,* and *I'm the King of the Castle!*

Hide and Seek by Arnold Shapiro.

A short book with durable cardboard pages about two young children playing hide-and-seek. On each page there is a flap to open to look for the hidden child. When not there, the word *no* shows as well. The high-interest contents about a popular game, the peekaboo flaps, and repetition of the word *no* which teaches it as reading vocabulary are excellent attributes of the book.

The School by John Burningham.

A short picture book with one sentence per page about all the things you do when you go to preschool or kinder garten. The other excellent books in the series include: *The Baby, The Snow,* and *The Rabbit.*

Where Did the Baby Go? by Sheila Hayes.

A young girl finds a baby picture of herself. By the end of the story she realizes that she was that baby and is now a big girl.

Baby Dear by Esther Wilkin.

When a mother brings her new baby home from the hospital, the first child is given a doll called Baby Dear to be her baby. She takes care of her doll in the same way her mother takes care of the baby.

The New Baby by Ruth and Harold Shane.

This book about a family getting ready to bring home a new baby focuses on preparing the first child to accept the new sibling.

Are You My Mother? by P. D. Eastman.

A story about a bird that is hatched while his mother was away from the nest. He goes around asking a lot of different animals and objects if they are his mother until he finds his own.

T.A. for Tots by Alvyn M. Freed, Ph.D.

Transactional analysis for the preschool child. This book with large print and pictures helps a child understand his feelings and accept himself as being "OK."

Educational

ABC Book illustrated by John Polak for Grossett and Dunlap.

Each page has a capital and lowercase letter of the alphabet in print and in cursive, a large clear picture of something that starts with that letter, and a clear printed word. It also includes ten illustrated numbers.

Counting Little Indians by Playmore Inc., Publishers.

A story on durable cardboard pages about ten little Indians doing different activities. Each page has one more Indian on it. The first page has one and the last has all ten. Other books in the series include: *Goldilocks and the Three Bears, The Frog Prince, Three Little Kittens, Cinderella, Jack and the Beanstalk, Hansel and Gretel,*

Snow White, Thumbelina, A.B.C. Book, Tell Me What Time It Is!, Little Red Riding Hood, Mother Goose, and *The Three Little Pigs.*

Ladybird Talkabout Books published by Ladybird Books Ltd., Loughborough, England, 1974.

In addition to its main purpose of increasing a child's vocabulary and understanding, the topics are educational. The pages are full of picture activities to play and talk about together. The following are in the series:

Talkabout Animals	*Talkabout Clothes*
Talkabout Home	*Talkabout the Park*
Talkabout the Beach	*Talkabout Gardens*
Talkabout Shopping	*Talkabout Starting School*
Talkabout Baby	*Talkabout Holidays*

How Come? Easy Answers to Hard Questions by Joyce Richards.

This book is created from the award-winning advertising campaign for Health-tex clothes in response to requests from parents and educators throughout the country. It is a compilation of selected advertisements seen in many newspapers and magazines.

Grover's Book of Cute Little Baby Animals by B. G. Ford.

Grover goes to the library to take out a book. He picks out a book about animals and their babies, and that story is told within this book. It has excellent photographs of mother and baby animals and teaches the proper names for them all.

My Doctor by Harlow Rockwell.

An excellent introduction to what doctors do. The pages have large print, simple sentences, and clear and interesting pictures. This appealing and accurate presentation will be excellent preparation for children who are going to a doctor. There are other books in this series that also provide an excellent foundation for experiences children will have in those areas. The titles are: *My Dentist, The Toolbox, The Thruway,* and *Machines.*

Telephones pictures by Christine Sharr for Grossett and
     Dunlap.
     A large-size book short in length that explains clearly
     how telephones work. It is an excellent, historical ap-
     proach that shows how they developed from early times
     and have advanced to include the many modern adapta-
     tions of today. Also included in the series is *Fire*, which is
     equally historical and informative about its topic.
Goodnight Moon by Margaret Wise Brown.
     A literary classic about going to bed. The pages even
     darken as the story progresses.
The Little Engine That Could by Watty Piper.
     A story about a train whose engine breaks down. He
     needs another one to carry all his goodies for young
     children to the other side of the mountain. Many engines
     will not bother, but finally an old one agrees to try and
     makes it.
Let's Read and Find Out Science Book Series published by
     Thomas Y. Crowell Company, New York, 1980.
     These are easy-to-read books that teach important con-
     cepts in simplified terms with clear illustrations. There
     are many; I suggest the following:

How a Seed Grows	*What Makes Day and*
My Five Senses	*Night*
Oxygen Keeps You Alive	*What the Moon Is Like*
Straight Hair, Curly Hair	*Your Skin and Mine*
What Happens to a Ham-	*The Skeleton inside You*
burger	*High Sounds, Low Sounds*

If you find you are reading some books over and over,
there are a couple of games you can play while you read. You
can leave out a word at the end of a sentence and see if your
child can fill it in. If not, after a short pause, fill it in yourself.
Be careful not to put him on the spot. Maybe after more
repetition another time he will be able to do it. Continue in
this manner with other words in the book.

Another game is to ask your child to listen for mistakes as you read. Have him say "stop" as soon as he hears you read a word wrong. If he misses it, you correct it and continue in the same manner.

READING BOOK

Objective
To give the child the satisfaction of successful reading.

About the Game
This activity can be adapted to any level. If the child is not reading at all, use a book with nice pictures and talk about them. If the child can do it with alphabet or number books, that is fine. If he can use some of the Dick Bruna books like *I Can Dress Myself, I Can Read, I Know about Numbers*, or others in that series, those are good. They are published by Methuen Inc., 733 Third Avenue, New York, New York 10017. *Hop on Pop* by Dr. Seuss and several others in his Beginner Books Series are often highly motivating. They are published by Random House, Inc., New York, New York. There is also a nice three-book series by Joan Walsh Anglund called *The Adam Book, The Emily Book,* and *The Adam and Emily Book of Opposites*, also published by Random House. The repetition of sentence structure leads to early reading success. The other alternative for this reading time are home-made books. You can take a small photo album and put pictures on one side and a descriptive word, phrase, or simple sentence on the other side. A personalized book like this about a trip or home activities is always of high interest to the child. You can also cut apart a coloring book, paste pictures from it on construction paper pages inserted in a three-ring binder and make up a story with words your child knows how to read. For these homemade books, you can use one word,

two words, three words, or short sentences, whichever is most appropriate.

How to Play
This is the time to share reading with the child on his own reading level. Choose a book that he will enjoy and that is easy enough for him to feel successful at, and alternate reading. You take all the left-hand pages and he the right-hand pages or vice versa. Always point out the words when you read your side.

CHILD'S MAGAZINE

Objective
To give the child a chance to go through one of his magazines with you.

About the Game
For this age range, I recommend *Sesame Street Magazine* (P.O. Box 2896, Boulder, Colorado 80321), *My Weekly Reader for Kindergarten* (Xerox Education Publications, 1250 Fairwood Ave., Columbus, Ohio 43216), and *Highlights for Children* (2300 West Fifth Avenue, P.O. Box 269, Columbus, Ohio 43216). Choose whichever you feel is most appropriate for your child. There are many activities in these that are designed for parent-child interaction and this is your special time for that interaction.

How to Play
Subscriptions to these are nice for a child. He will enjoy receiving monthly copies by mail. When they come, he can do what he can with them on his own. For this game time, focus on activities that will be especially interesting and/or helpful to your child. Reading one of the stories to him is also beneficial.

CATEGORIES BOOK

Objective
To help the child see and understand more about the complicated world in which we live and to help build his vocabulary.

About the Game
A simpler version of this book was suggested in *Teaching with
Toys*. If you have made that book, you can expand upon it. If
not, you can get a new three-ring binder and add construction
paper pages. Use a different color for each of the categories
and label the first page in a group clearly.

How to Play
Old *Sesame Street Magazine*s, other magazines with clear
colorful pictures, and store catalogs are sources for pictures
for the categories you have chosen. In addition, pictures from
food and toy boxes are excellent. Cut out pictures and place
them on colored paper in categories. Flowers, animals, people, food, toys, and the kitchen are good starters. Depending
on the age, ability, and interest of the child, he can make some
or most of this book. You can label each item in large letters
for easy reading.

Another way to make this kind of book is with an inexpensive photo album. Slip the selected pictures under the
protective plastic along with any labels you have made. Read
and discuss this book with your child at the appropriate level.
Again point out the words when you read.

LETTERS

Objective
To give your child the opportunity to learn the name and sounds of the letters while playing games.

About the Game
Make a set of alphabet cards from index cards. Put the capital letter on one side and the lowercase on the other. Hole punch one corner and loop a piece of yarn about eight inches long through the hole. On a sheet of poster board print the letters of the alphabet, capitals on one side and lowercase on the other. See how the letters are spaced in the illustration.

How to Play
You can use the alphabet cards like toys. Hang them on door knobs or in other places or hide them for play. Trace your finger around the letter in the way you would write it and show your child how to do the same. You can talk about the letter sounds and things that start with their sound. You can

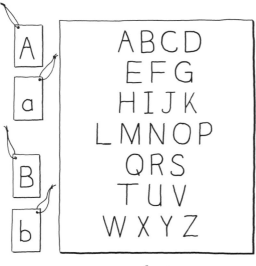

front

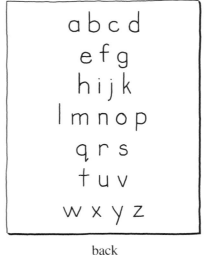

back

even hide something behind your back that starts with the sound of a letter and ask him to try to guess it. Try to use only one or two at a time. The next time you play, review the old and introduce one or two more. It is best not to ask direct questions like "What letter is that?" Saying things like "You have the B" or "I like your M for Mommy" is better. The alphabet chart is for singing the alphabet song. Point to the letters as you sing together. After you sing the ending, repeat the song and point to the lowercase letters on the back of the chart. Your child can do the pointing as well. Here are the words.

> A B C D
> E F G
> H I J K
> L M N O P
> Q R S
> T U V
> W X Y Z
> Now I've sung my ABCs
> Next time won't you sing with me?

Leave out the *and* between *Y* and *Z*. That could be confused with an *N*, and there is nothing to point to for that word.

You can also use the chart for a matching game. Take out the alphabet cards one at a time and ask your child to match it correctly on the chart. You can use both sides, matching capitals to capitals, lowercase to lowercase, or capitals to lowercase and lowercase to capitals.

WORD CARDS

Objective
To help the child build a sight vocabulary.

About the Game
There are one hundred words that are most frequently heard in the English language. These words make up 50 percent of all elementary school reading. The first ten make up 25 percent of all elementary reading. They are all printed in duplicate on pages 157–63 and can be cut out for playing several different games. For each game, start with a few words and add more as the child masters them.

How to Play
Concentration is an all-time favorite for children. You can start with three pairs and later play with as many pairs as is

the 1	he 11	at 21	but 31	there 41
of 2	was 12	be 22	not 32	use 42
and 3	for 13	this 23	what 33	an 43
a 4	on 14	have 24	all 34	each 44
to 5	are 15	from 25	were 35	which 45
in 6	as 16	or 26	we 36	she 46
is 7	with 17	one 27	when 37	do 47
you 8	his 18	had 28	your 38	how 48
that 9	they 19	by 29	can 39	their 49
it 10	I 20	word 30	said 40	if 50

will 51	some 61	two 71	my 81	long 91
up 52	her 62	more 72	than 82	down 92
other 53	would 63	write 73	first 83	day 93
about 54	make 64	go 74	water 84	did 94
out 55	like 65	see 75	been 85	get 95
many 56	him 66	number 76	call 86	came 96
then 57	into 67	no 77	who 87	made 97
them 58	time 68	way 78	oil 88	may 98
these 59	has 69	could 79	now 89	part 99
so 60	look 70	people 80	find 90	over 100

appropriate for your child. Place the pairs mixed up face down on the table. Have the child pick one, turn it over, read it, and then pick another. If it matches, he keeps the pair and goes again. If not, he turns them both over and you take a turn. You both try to remember where the cards are on the table. If he has trouble reading a word, you help. After repetition of the game, he will start to remember more and more words. The winner is the one with the most pairs.

Before or after playing *Concentration*, you might want to play a simple matching game. Lay out one set of cards and ask the child to match cards you give him one at a time. For the rest of the games, one set of cards is enough, but you can use two sets for additional repetition.

Another game is to place the word cards you have chosen in a pile face down. Take turns picking a card. He goes first. If he can read it, he keeps it. If not, he puts it at the bottom of the pile, and then it's your turn.

A third version is to place a few cards face up on the table and read them to the child, pointing to the cards as you read. Then say you will read and make a mistake. He must say "stop" when he hears the mistake. Then the child is the reader and does the same.

Still another version is to use the cards like flash cards. However, you tell your child not to say the word until you hide the card behind your back. In this way he has to remember it and thus build his visual memory skills. In addition, there is less pressure to be right because the focus of the game is on remembering what he saw and not on reading correctly.

HOP, JUMP, AND CLAP

Objective
To give the child the opportunity to develop a sight word vocabulary with verbs.

About the Game
This activity gives the child a chance to practice reading action words, while acting out the words reinforces recognition of them. The element of surprise by picking each word card from a pile adds to the fun.

How to Play
Start with three words—*hop*, *jump*, and *clap*. Write each one on an index card and place the cards in a pile. Take turns with the child picking a card and acting out the word. After he masters reading those three, add another. Each time you play, start with the ones already made. If he knows them well, add another verb. Suggested beginning words are *walk, run, jog, sleep, swim, talk,* and *sing*; but any your child will enjoy acting out are fine.

There are several other versions of this game that help to develop children's love for make-believe by giving them the opportunity to act things out. For example, you could make a set of cards with different names of occupations on them like *fire fighter, police officer, doctor,* etc. There is a nice book called *What Do You Do? Jobs in Your Neighborhood* by Emily Perl Kingsley, published by Western Publishing Company in conjunction with Children's Television Workshop, that gives a good introduction in a fun way to many different jobs that people do. You could also have cards with names of animals on them for making animal sounds and acting out the animals. You can also make phrases for doing jobs around the house. Choose activities that will teach your child to really help you like *set the table, wash the dishes, dust the furniture, sort the silverware, pair the socks,* etc.

THIS IS A . . .

Objective
To give the child the opportunity to develop a sight word vocabulary with nouns.

About the Game
This activity gives the child a chance to practice reading while playing a labeling game. The element of surprise by picking each word card from a pile adds to the fun.

How to Play
Start with three words—*sofa, chair,* and *rug.* Write each one on an index card and place the cards in a pile. Take turns with the child picking a card and placing it on the object named on the card in a living room or family room. After he masters reading these three, add another. Each time you play, start with the ones already made. If he knows them well, add another word that describes something else in the room. Suggested beginning words are *table, lamp, wall, door, plant, window,* and *desk*; but any item of interest in the room is fine.

After a room vocabulary is built up, there are a few variations of this game that are fun to play. One is asking the child to place the whole pile of word cards in their proper place. Another is placing the cards all mixed up in the room and asking the child to fix them. The most advanced version is to make three more word cards— *This, is,* and *a.* Put them out on the table. Take turns picking a card to place at the end of the sentence and reading the new sentence you have made. For this and any of the games in which you take turns with the child, you can ask him at any time whether he would like to do your turn as well. If he does, he will be getting more practice without realizing he is doing extra work. If he is happy to keep taking turns, that is fine too. Taking turns with a child is often what changes an activity from one he was unwilling to do into a pleasant interaction.

MESSAGE

Objective
To give the child the opportunity every day to read something interesting, personal, and at his own level.

About the Game
A good-quality wall blackboard or standing easel type and soft chalk are necessary to do this activity.

How to Play
On a blackboard placed eye level for a child, write an appropriate message for your child that he will be able to read. You can start with easy ones and get progressively harder. One example is, "Good morning, *(child's name)*. Have a good day." If it is interesting for your child, set up his desk where he can see the blackboard and ask him to copy his message. This will then be a writing as well as reading activity.

2

Games for Writing Development

Writing skills develop through practice combined with the proper amount of fine motor exercises. This chapter presents for the child different activities for writing practice, and chapter 9 suggests other ways to enhance fine motor development. Because eye-hand coordination is an important part of successful writing, many of these games include copying tasks.

Some of these games are available in workbooks found in school supply stores or discount stores. If they are prepared on the appropriate level for your child, they are fine; but often they are too difficult for a young child. She may be old enough to do the skill but only in a more simplified form.

COPY AND COLOR IN SHAPES

Objective
To give the child the opportunity to improve eye-hand co-ordination by copying a simple shape and then to improve her coloring ability by giving her a clear outline to color.

About the Game
Both copying and coloring are important developmental skills. As simple shapes are mastered, the task can be used with more difficult shapes, giving the child a chance to learn more about shapes as well.

How to Play
Fold an 8½″ × 11″ sheet of paper in four parts. Draw two shapes in the two upper sections. Ask the child to copy and color them in the two lower sections. Emphasize coloring in the whole shape. A more advanced version of the game would be to have the child draw the shapes on the top two sections and you copy and color them.

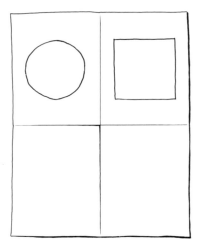

PICTURE COPYING

Objective
To give the child the opportunity to improve eye-hand co-ordination by copying a drawing.

About the Game
You can begin this game on a simple level and draw more advanced pictures with more detail as the child grows. A simple house with a tree and flowers is a good start, and a whole landscape can be developed at a future time if your artistic skills are up to it.

How to Play
Fold an 8½″ × 11″ sheet of paper in half. Draw a picture on the top half and ask the child to copy it on the bottom. As she is ready for more elaborate pictures, draw them with more detail. Another version of the game would be to have the child draw a picture, and you copy it.

FASHION PLATES OR VARIATION

Objective
To use a commercially prepared game for eye-hand coordination and coloring practice.

About the Game
You can buy in most toy stores a game called *Fashion Plates* by TOMY. The first part of the activity practices the skill of holding a paper steady and applying pressure with a special crayon set up sideways to make the design appear. This part of the activity is like doing a rubbing. The second part, once the rubbing has appeared, is to color it in with colored pencils or crayons.

How to Play
Have the child put together in the proper place the fashion outfit she chooses. Then have her place the paper over it. She then uses the sideways crayon to make her rubbing of the outfit. After that she colors in her own picture. Share in the activity in any natural way. There are also other versions of this game available that have more interesting designs for boys.

FOLLOW THE DOTS

Objective
To give the child a follow-the-dots exercise that is simple, clear, and designed for her level. This is a sequencing activity.

About the Game
You can make follow-the-dots patterns quickly and easily and at the correct level of difficulty for the child. You can use numbers or alphabet letters to label the dots. Good designs for the dots are numbers and letters themselves.

How to Play
Make a follow-the-dots paper for the child. Lead her through the activity as much as is necessary. Work toward independence in the activity. Again, the child can make some follow-the-dot exercises if she is able, and you can follow the dots.

TRACING

Objective
To give the child practice in the fine motor control of staying on the line with her pencil.

About the Game
There are different ways to do this activity depending on what materials are available to you. Tracing paper can be put over any coloring book page and fastened down with paper clips or stapled. There are also some coloring books that have tracing paper already inserted. If no tracing paper is available, you can use a plain coloring book page and have her use a crayon to go over the outlines of the picture.

How to Play
As with many of the activities, sharing is an important part of this one. Have her trace a line, and then you trace one. Alternate with her until all the lines on the page are covered. In addition, you can trace around objects like shapes cut from cardboard or index cards. The shape can be cut inside the card like a template or outside forming the card into the shape. You can also take turns tracing around easily accessible objects like blocks, cookie cutters, poker chips, and pieces from Tangrams or other geometrical shape sets.

FOLLOWING A MAZE

Objective
To give the child the opportunity to practice the fine motor control of staying within the lines of a path and also in a more advanced form to give her the opportunity to practice the thinking and planning necessary for following a maze.

About the Game

The children's magazines referred to in chapter 1 often have easy mazes. However, it is sometimes more fun to make your own. In that way you can tailor the difficulty to the level of your child. You can begin with a simple maze and make the maze more difficult as the child becomes ready.

How to Play

Draw a maze for the child. Ask her to get to the end without going out of the lines or crossing a line. The simplest can be a straight path, and the most complicated can be one with many choices. You can make up any story you like for this activity, such as "Help the dog find his bone," "Help the boy find his house," "Help the girl find her truck."

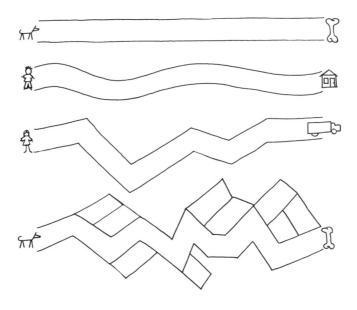

CROSSING OUT LETTERS

Objective
To give the child the opportunity to develop visual perception and to practice writing while playing a treasure hunt game.

About the Game
Find any lines of print of suitable size for your child or write your own sentences. You might want to start with large print and gradually use a smaller size.

How to Play
Put at least two lines of print in front of the child. Ask her to go on a treasure hunt for *a*'s and to put an *X* on all the *a*'s, both capital and lowercase, in the first line. Then ask her to go on a treasure hunt for a different letter in the next line. For example:

> Cynthia, you look pretty today.
> I like your new red dress.

Once she has the concept, you can ask her to find two or more letters in the same sentence. At the end you can ask her to copy either next to or under the sentence the letters not crossed out.

CHOOSING SHAPES FROM A GROUP

Objective
To give the child the opportunity to develop visual discrimination and to practice writing while playing a game.

About the Game
You can make this as hard or as easy as is appropriate for the child by varying the shapes and their sizes. Start off with easy

worksheets and then make more complicated ones as the child advances.

How to Play
Make a design with mixed shapes and ask the child to outline in a crayon or marker all the shapes of one kind first. For example, if there are circles, start with those. Then in a different color have her outline another shape and so on until all the shapes on that paper have been done. A more advanced version is to take a word and scramble the letters together. Then ask the child to identify the letters and write out the word correctly.

Another activity designed to develop the skill of discriminating by shape is *Sort O' Cards* described in *Teaching with Toys*. It teaches matching by shape, by color, and by number.

COLOR BY NUMBER

Objective
To give the child the opportunity to do a think-and-do activity emphasizing visual perception, as well as practice coloring within lines.

About the Game
You can use for the drawing anything with clear sections that can be numbered, or make a random design. Use two or three numbers in the beginning and make the designs more advanced as the child gains skill.

How to Play
For each number you use on your paper, write a key for the child to follow. You can also put a line in the proper color next to the color word to help the child. The child can do the activity, or you can take turns coloring different numbers.

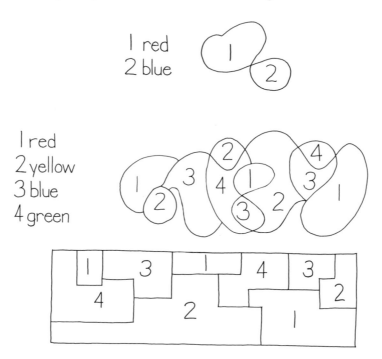

This is a detective type of activity, and you can ask her to be a good detective and find all the ones, twos, etc. As in other coloring activities, it is appropriate to emphasize coloring in the whole space and trying to leave no white space at all.

COPY A PATTERN

Objective
To give the child a beginning writing activity in addition to eye-hand coordination practice by copying.

About the Game
Start with simple patterns and do more advanced ones later. Make them according to the level and interest of the child.

How to Play
Fold an 8½″ × 11″ sheet of paper in half. Draw your pattern on the left-hand side. Start with a simple pattern. Have the child copy the pattern on the right-hand side of the page. If she is successful, make the next pattern a little more difficult. If not, use the same or an easier pattern. You can also describe the relationship of one item to the other as to the left, right, in front of, behind, next to, etc., and ask questions about the locations to help teach spatial relationships.

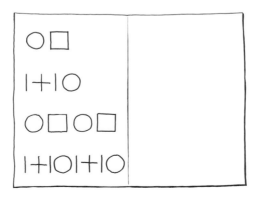

CHALKBOARD WRITING

Objective
To give the child an opportunity to practice writing in a situation where it is easy to erase. This activity will help a child who has a fear of making written mistakes.

About the Game
This exercise is best done with a chalkboard about 9″ × 12″ size or larger that can be laid out on a desk or table where the child works.

How to Play
Design an appropriate writing activity for the child: letters, numbers, words, or sentences. You write it across the top of the board and ask her to copy it below. Encourage her to be a good detective about her own work and erase and change any mistakes.

"SHOW ME" GAME

Objective
To teach the child that writing is a means of self-expression and also that wrong answers can be easily erased and corrected. This activity will help a child who has a fear of making written mistakes.

About the Game
The main activity for this game can be of your choice. Whatever type of answer your child will enjoy writing is fine: answers to equations, beginning sounds, a picture, or something else of your choice. Be sure the child's pencil has an eraser and that she feels free to erase any answer that is not right.

How to Play
Fold an 8½″ × 11″ sheet of paper in four parts. Number the sections 1, 2, 3, and 4. Ask the child a question. She is to write the answer in box number 1. After you ask the question, say, "Show me, don't tell me." This gives her a chance to directly use her writing as a means of communication. As with other games, you can do a version where she asks you a question. You write the answer and then show it.

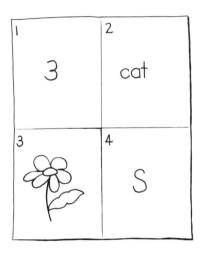

WRITING ON LINED PAPER

Objective
To give the child a chance to practice writing on her own level.

About the Game
Whatever the writing level of the child, this is the time for practice. If she can do letters, use letters, if words, do words, if sentences, use sentences.

How to Play
Try to get preschool paper. It is different from other paper because for every line of writing it has a heavy line that you can refer to as the hat line that is a guide for the top of the letter, another heavy line that you can refer to as the foot line that is a guide for the bottom of the letter, and a middle dotted line that you can call the belt line for the middle of the letter. If it is not available, make your own lines following the pattern in the illustration. You write the word or words on the first set of lines and have the child copy it on the next set. When she is done, write another row and have her copy that. If the child takes the initiative, she can write a row for you to copy.

LETTER WRITING

Objective
To give the child an opportunity to practice her writing as a communication skill.

About the Game
You can give the child as much or as little spelling help as she needs to get her message across.

How to Play
Check the next birthday or anniversary in your family, including grandparents, aunts, and uncles. Have the child write a letter. Guide the child as necessary. If you choose to write another kind of letter, a suggestion is to write one to you. You or she can address the envelope. She can fold the letter, put it in the envelope, seal it, and put a stamp on it. You can take her to a mailbox to mail it. She will be delighted to see it postmarked and come back to your house through the mail.

3

Games for
Language Development

Growth in speech helps us to express our thoughts, and growth in thoughts is reflected in our speech. Effective speech results from vocabulary acquisition as well as clear articulation. Therefore, language development results from multi-faceted inputs.

The following games deal with different aspects of language growth. They are geared to stimulate a child with delayed development and to help a child for whom language comes easily to enjoy and expand his skills.

PLAY AND SAY

Objective
To give the child the opportunity to answer questions in the context of an enjoyable rhyming poem.

About the Game
The first two lines are for participation. The next five are for listening. The last part is for pleasant interaction with you. Responses for beginning talkers should be one or two words, and those for more advanced speakers should be simple sentences and then paragraphs. This game is also in *Teaching with Toys.*

How to Play
The following is the text of the poem.

> Hello, what is your name?
> How old are you?
>
> Glad to meet you.
> Yes, it's true.
>
> Let's play a game that's fun to do.
> Listen to the words I choose.
> And tell me what it is you use.
>
> What do you drink from?
> What do you eat with?
> What is the food on?
> What do you like to eat?
> What do you like to drink?
> What do you like to play?
> What do you like to say?

Start by asking the first question. Wait for an answer. If the child is not ready to answer, you supply the answer for him. Then ask the second question following the same procedure. If he is not answering at first, he will at a later time. By playing this game often he will hear the answers many times and begin supplying them when he is ready. When you start line three, put out your hand for a handshake and start the "Glad to meet you" section of the poem.

The last part is for developing verbal expression. The beginning talker will give one-word answers. Later more words will come, and still later sentence and then paragraph answers.

After much repetition, you and the child will get to know this poem like an old friend. You can take it with you from memory wherever you go. It can be a diversion in a car ride, at the park, or in any place of your choice.

I SEE

Objective

To give the child the opportunity to expand verbal communication skills in the context of a game. It is also designed to increase visual perception and environmental awareness.

About the Game

In the home this game will expand awareness of the home environment, while outside it will broaden awareness of the world around. Anywhere it will stimulate the child to be a good detective for the things around him. Whether driving in a car, riding in a bus, waiting to be served in a restaurant, in the waiting room of a doctor's office, or sitting around at home, playing "I see" will enrich a child's language self-expression along with expanding environmental awareness.

How to Play

Taking turns with the child, say "I see . . . ." Begin by filling in a one-word answer and lead up to a more complicated sentence. For example, if playing in the living room, you might start with "I see a sofa." Later it might become, "I see a sofa with a pillow on it." Still later, "I see a sofa with a blue pillow on it with white dots. I also see a picture above it with four fish on it swimming in the water." The response should be appropriate for the child's language ability and can be played with two children on different levels of language.

WHO, WHAT, WHERE, WHEN, WHY

Objective
To give the child the opportunity to build his vocabulary and to learn to express himself better by developing his understanding of the five basic question words: *who, what, where, when,* and *why*.

About the Game
In the early days of print, books were few in number and were of great value to the people who owned them. Children's books were limited to nursery rhymes and fairy tales with few or no pictures. Today, besides the wealth of brightly colored children's books, we have an abundance of store catalogs, magazines, and children's magazines, all containing a wealth of pictures for vocabulary building. They are readily available for discussions and even to be cut apart and used in different ways by children, parents, and teachers.

How to Play
Choose any available magazine or catalog. Find a picture that you think might be appealing to the child. Discuss it in a way that stimulates thought, using the words *who, what, where, when,* and *why* as introductions. Ask such questions as, "Who is in the picture? What are they doing? Where do you think they might be going? When do you think they will be back? Are they happy and why or why not?"

An excellent source of pictures for this game are in a set of picture books without words by Helen Oxenbury. They are all short, have durable cardboard pages and tell stories with a good sense of humor about everyday occurrences for parents and children. The titles are: *Friends, Playing, Dressing, Working, Family, Mother's Helper, Beach Day, Monkey See, Monkey Do, Good Night, Shopping Trip.*

In addition to asking the five questions, you can ask the child to find specific details in a picture. Besides increasing vocabulary, this is an opportunity to improve visual perception.

DESCRIBE AN OUTFIT

Objective
To give the child the opportunity to develop self-expression.

About the Game
Clothes hanging in a closet are of high interest to children. Because they have different colors, patterns, and styles, they provide a subject with lots of descriptive words.

How to Play
Open up the child's closet and stand with him a few feet away. Ask him to choose an outfit by describing it. You then select the items of clothing based on his description. In the beginning his responses will be brief. Encourage him to be more specific and tell you more details so that you will be better able to pick out the items. Once this game technique has become fun and successful, you can use it together when you go to select the child's outfit for the day.

RHYMES

Objective
To give the child the opportunity to improve auditory perception.

About the Game
The age-old pastime of making rhymes has always held fascination for children. Dr. Seuss, the master of rhyming books for children, will live forever in the world of children.

How to Play
Make a set of flash cards out of index cards, one word on each side and the rhyme on the back. The following are suggested pairs: *man/tan, pan/fan, hop/top, mop/pop, car/far, tree/me, play/say, day/may, hat/cat, sit/hit*. Write each pair in a different color using marker or crayon. Choose a card from a pile and read the pair. Have the child take his turn. Help him with his rhyme if he has trouble in the beginning.

After playing for a while and gaining familiarity with the rhyming couplets, play by reading one side and guessing the rhyme on the back. Turn it over to check. If you have played this game a lot, you can then use the principle in a car, bus, or other location without cards and try to remember rhymes from the cards or be able to make up some new ones.

WORD MEMORY

Objective
To give the child the opportunity to develop short-term memory.

About the Game
An age-old game for memory development is "I packed my suitcase." There are different versions of this you can play depending on the age and ability of the child.

How to Play

Using the traditional format, you can start, "I packed my suitcase and in it I put . . ." The first person completes the sentence with an *A* word like *apple*. The second person says the same sentence, uses the *A* word and adds a *B* word. For example, "I packed my suitcase and in it I put an apple and a banana."

A simpler version of the game for a younger child could be just to use words with no introductory sentence and without alphabetical order, or to use the introductory sentence but play the game without alphabetical order. You can also use the format of the game with no introductory sentence, just categories like clothes, food, flowers, or animals. For example, if clothes is the category, the child starts with a word like *dress*. You add to it by saying "dress" and something like "coat." He says, "dress, coat" and something like "shoe" and so on. When the list gets too long and he cannot repeat it, start again either with the same category or a different one.

A still simpler version of this memory-building game is to use random words. Say three like "shoe, car, tree" and have the child repeat them. Then pick another three. When he is good at remembering three, try sets of four words. When he does fine with four-word groups, go on to five and so on.

SPELL A WORD

Objective

To give the child the opportunity to practice spelling using high-interest words.

About the Game

While spelling might seem like an advanced skill, children can learn to spell high-interest words at a very young age. You can get the spiral-bound index card notebook used in this game in the stationery department of most discount stores.

How to Play

Choose for the child whatever word you and he pick. Good beginning words are *mommy, daddy, me, no, yes,* the child's name, any brother's or sister's names, *ice cream, you, love, I, dear, like, my, book,* and *toy.* As you can see from the selected list, this spelling skill will give the child the ability to be able to write independently and correctly a simple letter. Write one of the words on the first page of a spiral-bound index card notebook. Say the word, spell it, and say it again. Ask the child to do the same. Then cover it up with your hand and say and spell the word again. Next let him look at the word, cover it up, and take his turn again. Go back and forth with him until he has learned to spell it. Use just one word. Next time review that word. If he knows it, add another one on the next page of the notebook. Each time you play, continue to review all the previous words. Add another only if he can easily spell all the ones already in the notebook. An index card notebook is good for this activity because it is easy to take it with you on trips or errands. You might want to write a title on the cover. You can also use index cards, if just for home use. These can be held together with a rubber band or stored in an envelope.

WRITE A WORD FOR SPEECH

Objective
To help the child better pronounce certain words that he does not say clearly.

About the Game
I discovered this technique when my daughter came home from preschool singing "The Farmer in the Dell," but I could never make out that last word. When I corrected her with "Dell," she answered with her own version. This went on and on until I thought of writing it out. With all of her experience with letters and their sounds, she easily learned to say "Dell." This is a particularly helpful game for correcting words that have an abstract meaning.

How to Play
Select whatever word the child says incorrectly. Write it out for him on an index card or piece of paper. Read it several times and have him repeat it several times. Keep it for the next time you play this game. First show the new one and then review the old ones. Continue using all the words for a while after they have been mastered just for the reinforcement.

YES GAME

Objective
To give the child practice saying any word that he finds difficult to pronounce correctly.

About the Game
The word *yes* is good to start with because many children have trouble with its *s* sound. Some omit the *s* sound, and others stick their tongue out for it and make it sound like *th*. Others have trouble because they say "yeah" or other short-

cuts. Because the word will turn up for the child in a surprise way, he will enjoy his opportunity to say it. This is fun for him and has a more positive impact than correcting him when he says something wrong.

How to Play
Take six or seven index cards and write the word *yes* on each one. Place them in different places around the house. Whenever he sees one, he should say the word *yes*. After he has learned to say *yes* correctly, replace the cards with different cards that have another word that he has difficulty saying correctly. Continue with other words. This game improves reading as well as pronunciation. If speech pronunciation is not a problem for your child, choose other words that you would like to have him learn to read.

4

Games for Listening and Thinking Development

In a traditional classroom setting, teachers of readiness and beginning learning skills concentrate on developing for their students auditory discrimination, auditory memory, visual discrimination, and visual memory skills. They are all important in learning to read, write, do mathematics, and reason. The following games build those skills through activities that are easy to do around the house and are fun for the child.

HIDE THE TIMER OR THE MUSIC BOX

Objective
To give the child the opportunity to improve auditory discrimination skills while playing a game.

About the Game
A kitchen timer that has a ticking sound when set or a small music box like one that might have been part of a baby mobile can be used for this game. Any other musical toy or sound toy would work well too.

How to Play
Take turns with the child. Start by hiding a wound-up timer, music box, or sound toy. Have the child try to find it by following the sound. Once she finds it, she can hide it for you to find.

TAP A PATTERN

Objective
To give the child the opportunity to improve auditory discrimination and auditory memory skills while playing a game.

About the Game
This is a music readiness activity that helps children learn to hear a beat. It requires no materials but a table top. If that is not available, clapping the pattern is fine.

How to Play
Tap on the table once and have the child tap after you. Then tap twice and have her repeat that tap. Then tap three times and have her repeat that. If three times is the hardest she can do, stop with that and practice it several times. If three taps goes well, try three in a pattern like long, short, short or short,

short, long. Continue with expanded patterns that are appropriate for the child. You can do some with syllables like *valentine* for long, short, short or use the child's name.

SIMON SAYS

Objective
To give the child the opportunity to develop auditory discrimination and auditory memory in the context of a game.

About the Game
This is one of the age-old games that helps children learn to listen and follow directions. You can begin this game without the additional rule of not following the direction when the caller does not say "Simon says." When the child or group of children is ready, you can add that more complicated rule.

How to Play
The caller, an older child or you, says, "Simon says, touch your . . ." and fills in the sentence with a part of the body. She continues play with many more parts of the body. She can also change the format to action commands such as "Simon says jump, stand on one foot, hop," and more. The children playing follow each direction. If using the regular rule, the children are not to follow the direction if the caller does not say "Simon says."

CARRY OUT COMMANDS

Objective
To give the child the opportunity to improve auditory discrimination and auditory memory while following directions in the context of a game format.

About the Game
You can start with two directions and go on to three, four, or five, depending on the level of the child. The directions are to do actions which children enjoy.

How to Play
Give the child a few directions to follow and ask her to do them in the order given. For example, "Touch the table and then the refrigerator " or "Touch the chair and then the sofa and then the carpet." Another way to do it would be, "Clap your hands, jump over a card, and then walk around me." When you ask them to do activities that involve positioning their bodies in relation to objects—on, over, under, around, in, etc.—you are also helping them to develop perception of position in space and spatial relationships. A variation of this game is to ask the child to write a sequence of symbols like a question mark, a specific letter, and a specific number. Any figures the child can write are appropriate.

CALL TIME

Objective
To give the child the opportunity to improve auditory discrimination and auditory memory by hearing a spoken paragraph and being able to focus in on a small detail.

About the Game
In every area there is a local telephone number one can dial to get the correct time. You can get that number from informa-

tion. The telephone is an appealing medium to bring language to a child. A more advanced child can dial the number herself. This is also good for a child learning to practice dialing because she can have the success of dialing a number without bothering someone on the other end to answer the phone. In addition, learning to read a number from left to right and then finding the correct numbers on the telephone practices both visual memory, left-to-right progression, and eye-hand coordination.

How to Play
Dial the local number for the time and ask your child to listen for the time and then tell it to you. Since it is given as part of a longer message, she must listen carefully for the time, not knowing exactly where in the message she will hear it.

STRINGING BEADS IN THE ORDER DIRECTED

Objective
To give the child the opportunity to improve auditory memory along with the opportunity to develop a fine motor skill.

About the Game
Because colorful beads are often easily accessible in the home of a small child, the medium is good for a directions-following activity. You can start with a direction for two beads and expand to three, four, or five, as the child is ready. If beads are not available, you can use painted noodles, colored empty spools, or something else you find for stringing.

How to Play
Tell the child to string the beads in a certain order. For example, "String the blue bead and then the red." Later your direction can be changed to include three, like "First the yellow, then the blue, then the red." Keep adding commands up to a level of difficulty appropriate for your child.

MEMORIZING

Objective
To give your child the opportunity to improve her memory and learn something interesting and fun at the same time.

About the Game
Choose any poem that you think your child will enjoy. If you do not know one by heart that you love, look in a children's anthology of poetry, any handy collection of children's verse, or a book of Mother Goose rhymes.

How to Play
Teach the poem to your child one couplet or one four-line verse at a time. Say it and ask her to repeat it. Keep going over the same lines until she knows them by heart. The next time you play, review the old lines and then add the next grouping.

STORY OF THE DAY

Objective
To give the child the opportunity to improve her memory, learn some information, and to develop listening and thinking skills.

About the Game
Because the most interesting story a child could hear is one about herself and because information for this kind of story is readily available, a story about the child's own experiences during the day is fun and easy to tell. Bedtime is an excellent time for this activity. It is a nice way to end the day because it recaps for the child the events of the day. It can also include information about what she will do the next day and therefore prepare her for exciting coming events. It develops for the child a sense of time by establishing the past, present, and future.

How to Play

Begin the story in the same way each time. "Once upon a time" is the traditional story opener, but you can make up others like "This is the story of the day of (*Name*)" or "On (*date*) (*Name*) woke up, saw the daylight, and hugged her mom and dad." You can also repeat in this story the child's address, phone number, birthday, and any other facts that you would like her to learn. Then go on to tell the events of the day. She can participate in the story at whatever level of language she has. It is also an opportunity to discuss any events of the day that might have been either particularly troublesome or exceptionally happy.

STORY OF THE BODY

Objective

To give the child the opportunity to improve her memory, learn some concepts, and to develop listening and thinking skills.

About the Game

Because the most important topics to people are about things that relate to themselves, a story about how their bodies work is of high interest. Telling these around mealtime, bedtime, and potty time is helpful because it gives added meaning to those activities. For children who resist eating, using the bathroom, or going to bed, this game explains to them why these activities are good for them. They become not just something their parents say they have to do, but something with a purpose.

How to Play

For the story of the body start with information about food. The idea is to encourage proper eating habits. Explain to the best of your ability the four basic food groups and the importance of a balanced diet to making the body work well. Tell about how food first enters the mouth and is then chewed. Explain that when the pieces become small enough they move down a long pipe called the esophagus to the stomach. Show with your hand how the stomach chews it some more and breaks down pieces so small that they can travel through the body. Develop the idea that we eat during the day to give us energy to do our activities. Explain that we eat three times a day to keep providing fuel for our bodies while we are active and that we eat a little at each meal to keep us going until the next meal instead of eating too much at any one time.

For a child who resists using the toilet, telling the next part might be helpful. When you explain that the good parts or nutrients nourish the body, give it energy, and help it grow as they travel to every cell, and that the bad parts or wastes come out in the urine and bowel movements, she may be more willing to actively go to the toilet and let go of parts not good for her body.

A child resisting bedtime might stop resisting when she understands how helpful sleep will be to her ability to do daily activities well. Describe the nighttime as a time when we do not eat, as rest time for the body, which worked hard all day. It is when the body repairs some cells that were used during the day and builds some new ones to be ready for the next day.

An excellent reference for this topic, written in simple form, is a book called *Food and Digestion* by Brian Ward (Franklin Watts, Inc., 387 Park Avenue South, New York, New York 10016). Besides going over the basic sequence of digestion, it has a chapter on vitamins, one on each part of the digestive process, and one on each organ involved. It will enable you to enrich the basic story to whatever degree you feel appropriate for your child. There are also other books in this Human Body Series that you might also find helpful: *The Brain and Nervous System, The Ear and Hearing, The Eye and Sight, The Heart and Blood, The Lungs and Breathing,* and *The Skeleton and Movement.*

STORY OF THE PEOPLE

Objective
To give the child the opportunity to improve her memory, learn some concepts, and to develop listening and thinking skills.

About the Game
Because the most important topics to people are about things that relate to themselves and because the children at this stage have passed over the "Terrible Twos" transition time from being a baby to being a child, an independent person, they have high interest in topics that explain to them what people are like. Because they can now begin to develop goals, aspirations, and direction for their future, it is a good time to provide them with information about the jobs, activities, and interests of adults. It is even appropriate to explain to them on the proper level how they were born and how people have babies.

How to Play
For the first part take every opportunity to explain what you and your spouse do as work. If one or both of you earn money when you work, explain that concept too. As they get to know other adults, explain what they do to earn a living. Then as you take them to use various services in the community, explain the jobs of those people and how they earn money to support their familes by doing those jobs.

For the second part I recommend the book *How Babies Are Made* by Andrew C. Andry and Steven Schepp (New York: Time-Life Books, 1968). You can read a little at a time and discuss the ideas together. It has excellent clear pictures that explain reproduction on a child's level. It starts first with the reproduction of plants, goes on to animals, and then to people. Use it like any other story and let your child get this information from you. It will be helpful to her in her quest to understand herself as a person.

CHOOSING OBJECTS IN A ROOM

Objective
To give the child the opportunity to develop visual discrimination while playing a game.

About the Game
This activity is related to figure-ground discrimination. It develops the child's ability to be more aware of details in her environment.

How to Play
Sit together on a comfortable couch or set of chairs, indoors or out. Ask the child to find one category of objects like round things, green things, wooden things, etc. Then ask for more specific things like a book, picture, or chair. As the game continues, ask for less and less conspicuous items. You can also play the whole game with items in shapes.

CHOOSING OBJECTS FROM A GROUP

Objective
To give the child the opportunity to develop visual discrimination while playing a game.

About the Game
This activity is related to figure-ground discrimination. It develops the child's ability to pick things out of a large group. It also provides an opportunity to develop sorting skills and fine motor pincer grasp.

How to Play
Get a group of small items like paper clips, buttons, and rubber bands. Mix them all together on a table. Ask the child to find first all the paper clips, then the buttons, and then the

rubber bands. You can try it again in a different order. You can also go on to sorting the items into three different containers emphasizing picking up each item with the thumb and forefinger to develop pincer grasp at the same time. In addition, sorting by other characteristics like size, color, shape, and texture will further develop the skill.

WHAT'S MISSING?

Objective
To give the child the opportunity to develop visual memory while playing a game.

About the Game
This game can be played with anywhere from six to a dozen objects. Any simple small objects from around the home can be used, like a rubber band, paper clip, button, cotton ball, crayon, rock, etc. The more interesting they are to the child, the more successful the game will be.

How to Play
Put the selected number of items out on a tray or table surface. Ask the child to cover her eyes. Then remove the tray and take away one of the objects. Return the tray. When the child opens her eyes, ask "What's missing?" Next, you close your eyes and ask the child to remove an object. Then when you open your eyes, try to guess what she has removed.

A variation of the game to develop visual sequences is to have the child remove one object from the tray and then replace it in the same place she took it from. For the next turn you or she remove two objects, the same one and one more, and then replace both in their original places. Keep playing and increase the number of objects each time. Continue increasing to an appropriate number for the child.

VISUALIZATION

Objective
To give the child the opportunity to develop visual memory while playing a game.

About the Game
This game can be played with any symbols the child recognizes. It can also be used to teach one or two new symbols like letters, numbers, or words.

How to Play
Show the symbol to the child on an index card or small piece of paper. Tell her not to say it until you hide it behind your back. After it is hidden, she may say it. If you are using a symbol new to the child, tell her first what it is before you hide it.

A variation of the game is to describe a simple picture and then ask the child to draw it. For example, "a blue vase has three flowers in it, one large red one and two small yellow ones." Tell her to visualize in her mind what she is going to draw before she starts.

I SEE . . . AND DISCUSS

Objective
To give the child the opportunity to develop her thinking.

About the Game
This is an in-depth version of the *I See* game described in chapter 3. Besides the benefit of developing visual discrimination and increasing environmental awareness, it is designed to stimulate abstract thinking.

How to Play
Taking turns with the child, say "I see . . ." and have the child fill in the blank with the name of an object in the room. A one-word answer, such as "I see a sofa," is fine. This part is just like the *I See* game described in chapter 3. However, for this activity, discuss with the child her answer and have her expand upon her response. The idea is that through conversation the child will gain a deeper understanding of the things in her environment. Questions to help the child talk and think more about the object could be something like, "What is a sofa used for? What else is used for sitting? Why is a sofa helpful in a living room? What kinds of activities take place in a living room? What is another name for a sofa or a two-seated sofa?"

THE TIME CENTER

Objective
To give your child the opportunity to develop a sense of time.

About the Game
There are a few components to this system that will present to your child different ways we measure time. You can buy a 365-page calendar in a stationery story. The other wheels and charts you can make out of whatever you have handy. You can get any supplies you may need in a stationery store or a discount, drug, five-and-ten, or home supply store. Paper plates work well for the wheels. Construction paper strips covered with clear contact paper can be used for the clock hands and the pointer. Poster board is good for the charts with 8" × 10" index card pockets and cards. These can be attached by small brass prong fasteners. For extra durability, all charts and cards can be covered with clear contact paper. The same kind of fasteners attached loosely are good as hooks for hanging the cards on the chart. Picture hangers, as shown, would also work.

How to Play

Start with the Seasons Wheel (see illustration). Check it or reset it correctly. Then set the clock to the closest hour, half hour, or quarter hour, depending on how much your child knows about the clock. Then go on to the 365-page calendar. Have your child tear off yesterday's day and read the one for today. In the beginning show how the whole calendar has 365

Pocket to store
day cards

Pocket to store
month cards

days. As time goes, show how the year is coming to a close. By tearing one sheet each day, she will get the idea of the concept of a year.

Go to the large "Today is" chart. Ask your child to remove yesterday's day card, place it in the "Days of the Week" pocket and then choose from that pocket the proper day card and place it on the hook. Then ask her to choose from the pocket of the "Month" chart the proper month card and place it on the hook. Change the month card and update the year with a new calendar as appropriate. Use these wheels and charts every day or as little or as much as it remains interesting to your child. Help your child do the activities as little or as much as necessary.

ASSOCIATION

Objective
To give the child the opportunity to develop her thinking by seeing how things in her environment are related.

About the Game
Depending on what you choose, you can make the activity as simple or as complicated as you like. As you look around, you may find objects that through association will become more meaningful to the child. Besides the benefit of developing auditory memory, this activity is designed to stimulate abstract thinking.

How to Play
Start with simple associations until the child develops a clear concept of how to play. One starter might be, "You sit on a chair; you lie down on a _____ ." "Bed" is the answer. Here are a few more examples:

"You jump with your feet; you clap with your _____ ."

"In the morning you eat breakfast; in the afternoon you
eat _____ ."

"With your eyes you see; with your ears you _____ ."

Continue to make up as many as your child continues to enjoy. With practice she will catch on to the concept and be able to do more.

PLANNING

Objective
To give the child the opportunity to develop her thinking by imagining different situations.

About the Game
In the beginning try to choose situations that the child has experienced. After you are both used to this game, you can talk about situations that a child might have to face some time in the future like moving, trying a new sport, or even taking a trip into outer space.

How to Play
Introduce the game by descriptive sentences: "Let's pretend we are going on a picnic now. What do we need to take along?" Then write down on a sheet of paper the items as she and you mention them. The child can even draw a picture of the event after you both have planned it. Other topics that are good for planning are trips by car and plane, going out in the rain, playing a game, or even something simple like going to school.

5

Games for Midline Development

Crossing the midline of the body is an important skill for learning. Being able to easily reach an object with your right hand on the left side of your body and with your left hand on the right side is an important prerequisite for reading and writing. You must cross the midline of your body with your eyes to read and with your hands to write. Often children who are delayed in showing a hand preference need practice in this area. Those children who find it difficult to take things on the right side with their left hand and on the left side with their right hand need practice in using their hands to cross the midline of their bodies. Beginning ability to cross the midline starts to develop when a child is a few months old and is continually being refined. Hand preference starts to show up at about two years of age, and hand dominance is usually established by about the age of five.

There are many activities in normal child development that relate to this midline development. Crawling, which usually starts somewhere between six and nine months, practices a cross patterning movement. Tricycle and then bicycle riding also develops a body balance that works on this same midline development.

There are many midline exercises that are part of traditional physical education programs: in the lying down position with arms spread apart, leg stretches from the right side to the left arm and vice versa; in the sitting position with legs spread apart, arm stretches to opposite toes; in the standing position with feet spread apart, toe touching with opposite hands. There are many more. Some rely on the body to be aligned by the midline like sit-ups, push-ups, jumping jacks, and more. When directing a child in most basic exercises, or even yourself, keep in mind that the body should be midline centered with the head facing forward.

MIDLINE MATCHING

Objective
To give the child the opportunity to develop midline awareness by matching pictures that meet with each other vertically and horizontally.

About the Game
You can use easily accessible pictures from magazines for this activity or make your own drawings. Some lend themselves well to being cut vertically like faces, a lamp or bowl, a whole person, and other symmetrical pictures. Others can be cut horizontally like a house, a car, or almost anything long enough for placing the parts one on top of the other.

How to Play
Have pictures cut in two, some vertically and some horizontally. Ask the child to match the two parts. Start with the vertical tasks.

CHECKERBOARD PATTERNS

Objective
To give the child the opportunity to develop midline awareness by being able to match a pattern on the right side that he sees on the left side.

About the Game

You can play this with many variations and progress to harder rules and harder patterns as the child grows.

How to Play

With an open checkerboard and checkers in front of you, place a few checkers in squares on your side of the board. Have the child place checkers in the corresponding squares on his side. Add one to your side and ask him to place a corresponding one on his side. Continue the game as much as you feel is appropriate or clear the board and start again. You can also take turns who starts. Once the pattern is complete, you can talk about the positions of different checkers with descriptive words like *left, right, in front of, behind, next to,* etc., to help teach left and right and spatial relationships. When your child is ready you can go on to teach him how to play checkers.

YARN OVER HEAD AND ACROSS

Objective

To give the child an opportunity to develop midline awareness through his neck and with his eyes.

About the Game

A short piece of yarn or ribbon, about nine to twelve inches long, can be used for this activity. A flashlight can also be substituted for the yarn. The important part of the activity is the proper head movement.

How to Play

Have the child sit up straight on the floor. Kneel down behind him. Start with the yarn directly over his head. Have him lift his head straight up to look at it and then move the yarn slowly from left to right over his head. Ask him to follow it with his eyes. Encourage him to keep his eyes on the yarn and follow it all the way across, crossing the midline of his body with his eyes. If using a flashlight, project the light on a wall in front of him and have him follow it from left to right with his eyes.

ROLL A SMALL BALL

Objective
To give the child the opportunity to develop midline awareness by moving his eyes along the midline of his body.

About the Game
This game relates back to an old-time activity. Children have always enjoyed rolling balls to each other. A Ping-Pong ball or even a smaller one like one from a set of jacks or a paddle game is good. To accurately roll it, it must go slowly. The child then gets the built-in practice of following it with his eyes.

How to Play
Sit about four feet away from the child with your feet apart. Ask him to open his feet too. You can judge the proper distance by what feels comfortable for you both. Then roll the ball back and forth as straight as possible between you. Watch the ball as it rolls to you and ask the child to watch it when it rolls to him. Whoever rolls should look straight ahead at the other person before starting.

EYE EXERCISE

Objective
To give the child the opportunity to develop midline awareness by moving his eyes across the midline of his body and to strengthen the eye muscles as well.

About the Game
This activity is especially helpful to a child with weak muscles in his eyes. It will help him focus better. At first some children will need extra help keeping their heads still while moving just their eyes.

How to Play
With the child sitting opposite you, ask him to look at your face. Then show some of your fingers on the right side of his body and ask him to say how many there are. Ask him to move only his eyes to that side, not his head. Take the ones on the right side away and show some on the left. Again ask him to identify the number of fingers by moving his eyes and not his head. Repeat showing fingers from side to side and asking him to look at them by moving his eyes and not his head.

CROSS THE MIDLINE

Objective
To give the child the opportunity to develop midline awareness with his hands and arms and also to help him develop hand dominance.

About the Game
This is a game that can be fun for almost any child. Because it is a simple task, you can do it faster and faster to keep the interest of the child. A small ball or other small object of interest can be what is passed from side to side.

How to Play

Hold the small ball or object on the left side of the child's body. Also hold down his left hand so that he must take it with his right hand. Retrieve the ball or object and place it on the right side of the child's body. Hold down the right hand and ask him to get it with his left hand. Repeat the activity over and over for several minutes. You and he will get some silly laughs. He may even want to try it with you. Why not!

ARMS TOGETHER SIDE TO SIDE

Objective

To give the child the opportunity to develop midline awareness by moving his arms together from side to side across the midline of his body and to help develop hand dominance.

About the Game

Any object can be used that can be grasped by the child comfortably with two hands. At first you will need to hold the child's head still. Later he will be able to keep his own head straight.

How to Play

Place an object like a ball or can in the child's hands and have him clasp it securely in front of him. Then ask him to swing it from side to side across the midline of his body without moving his head. Ask him to look straight ahead at you with his head still and not to look at his waving arms. He should be able to feel the momentum of his arm movements. You can also do the arm swings opposite him to make the activity more fun.

Because this type of arm swinging is difficult, you can begin this activity by opening your arms and swinging them that way. The important part is that you keep your head straight. Again, you both can do this together. You will see that if you concentrate on moving at your waist, it will be easier. In addition, you will be doing an excellent waist exercise.

JACK-IN-THE-BOX

Objective
To give your child the opportunity to develop midline awareness by crossing the midline of his body with his hands and arms while acting out a rhyme.

About the Game
This is a short rhyme which if acted out properly helps to develop midline awareness while a child is having fun. For different ages, you can act this out in different ways. Here are the words and their accompanying motions.

Words	*Actions*
Jack in the box. Jack in the box.	Move left arm in a circle around the front of the body. (Repeat.)
Open the lid	Move left arm across the body and slowly cross it back. Bend down as it comes over.
And up he(she) pops.	Jump up.

Repeat the rhyme using the right arm.

How to Play
Stand opposite your child. As you say the words, explain the corresponding actions. Show him how to take his left hand and cross it over in front of his body straight to the right side. As you say, "Jack in the box," show him how to make it circle around to the left side and go back again in front of his body on the right side. Repeat. Do the same motion as you say,

"Open the lid," but this time tell him to bend down as his arm comes back to the right side. Then when you say, "And up he(she) pops," tell him to jump up. Explain that he will be doing the song twice, once with each arm. Do the singing and motions of the song together. Help him as much as is necessary to do the proper movements.

LEG AND ARM BALANCE

Objective
To give the child the opportunity to develop midline awareness by balancing and also to develop hand dominance by the cross patterning of the body.

About the Game
The mental process behind being able to lift an opposite arm and leg is an important part of this exercise. You must be midline centered in order to accomplish the balance.

How to Play
Get down on the floor on all fours with your child and do the exercise opposite him. First lift your left leg and your right arm and ask him to do the same. After maintaining your balance in that position, switch sides and lift your right leg and your left arm. Have him do that too. Both of you should try to maintain your balance for five to ten seconds. You can do this several times if you wish. With practice you will both be able to hold the positions longer.

If it is too difficult to maintain balance in the beginning, you can modify the game to start. Instead of lifting the opposite arms and legs, lift the same arms and legs. When you and he become comfortable with that, begin working with the opposite sides. Another idea to help beginning balance is to hold hands as you each lift your arms in the air. As your balance improves you can release your hands.

BODY MIDLINE STRENGTH

Objective
To give the child the opportunity to develop midline awareness by being centered by his trunk and also to strengthen those trunk muscles.

About the Game
This activity is especially helpful for a child with weak muscle tone. It will work to strengthen large muscles important for proper posture. It will also help to develop general body awareness which will be beneficial to all children.

How to Play
Sit the child across from you on a carpeted floor. Push on his chest with your hand as if to try to push him over. Ask him to push forward against your hand to keep his balance. Then from behind push his back forward. Ask him to push backward against your hand, again to keep his balance. Then push his body to the right at his left arm side and have him push left to maintain his balance. Do the same on the right side. You can repeat all four pushes with him several times. Tell the child what you are going to do and what you expect him to do before you begin each time. It is important that you and he understand the whole exercise.

ROW, ROW, ROW YOUR BOAT

Objective
To give your child the opportunity to develop midline awareness by moving back and forth while singing a song.

About the Game
This is fun because you do it together with your child and sing at the same time. The more you let your child pull you, the

more arm exercise he will get. The straighter you both stay as you move back and forth, the more effective the exercise will be.

How to Play
Sit opposite each other on the floor. Open your legs wide and have him place his legs inside yours. Join hands and move back and forth to the words of the song "Row, Row, Row Your Boat." You can go faster each time you sing, but do not go so fast that his neck muscles will jerk backward.

PAT-A-CAKE

Objective
To give your child the opportunity to develop midline awareness with his hands and arms while singing a song.

About the Game
This is one version of an age-old children's song passed down from generation to generation that provides exercise for the hands and arms. The more practice the child has with the song, the better he will be able to do the movements. The easiest motion for the beginning of the rhyme is clapping, but when he is ready you can show him how to cross clap with you. In that way he will also have the opportunity to cross the midline of his body with his hands. Here are the words and their corresponding motions.

Words	*Actions*
Pat-a-cake, pat-a-cake, baker's man,	Clap or cross clap several times.
Bake me a cake as fast as you can.	Continue to clap or cross clap.
Roll it,	Move your arms around and around each other.

And stir it,	Place hands together in front of you and move them around in a clockwise direction.
And mark it with a (*child's initial*),	Use your forefinger to mark the first initial of your child's name on your palm. Have your child mark the initial on his palm.
And toss it in the oven for (*his name*) and me.	Make a tossing motion with your hands.

How to Play

Sit opposite your child and do the singing and motions of the song together. Help him as much as is necessary to do the proper movements. For clapping you each clap separately. For cross clapping you each do one clap on your own and then extend your right hands to meet and clap. Then you each do another clap on your own and then extend your left hand to meet. Then repeat. The rest of the motions are more directly acting out the concept of the rhyme.

6

Games for Game-Playing Development

Children have a long time ahead of them as game players. There are a few characteristics of all games that can be learned that will enable a young child to be able to begin board and card games. Once the simple skills of basic games are mastered, children can then go on to master more complicated games at a later time. Sometimes a game you can purchase for a few dollars is the best way to introduce the techniques, and other times a game you can make quickly with easily accessible materials is better.

As part of teaching game-playing skills, you can teach some ideas about good sportsmanship. Some basic phrases you can teach by repetition for the fun of the words as well as for their meaning are,

> "It doesn't matter if you win or lose, it's how you play the game."
> "If at first you don't succeed, try, try again."
> "What happens when you fall down? You pick yourself up and keep going."

LOTTO

Objective

To give the child the opportunity to develop her ability to match while playing a competitive game.

About the Game

You can purchase at most toy stores simple picture matching games. They usually include about six boards with six pictures on each board, and there are playing cards to be piled in the center. You can also make your own board cards and matching playing cards with stickers, colored shapes, letters, numbers, words, etc.

How to Play

Each player picks a playing board. Then each player in turn picks a playing card from the pile. If it matches a picture on her card, she places it on the match. If it does not, it goes back to the bottom of the pile. The first player to complete matches for her whole card wins.

DOMINOES

Objective

To give the child the opportunity to develop her ability to match while learning to play an interactive game.

About the Game

If using a store-bought game with dots, choose either a large set or one in which the dot combinations are color coded. There are also store-bought versions specially made for young children on cards that have pictures for matching.

How to Play

Place a double domino, one with a matching set of dots on each side, in the center of the playing area. From the pile of face-down dominoes, each player will choose five to keep face up in front of her. If the first player has a domino that matches on one side the one in the playing area, she places that matching side next to it. If she has none that match, she chooses from the pile of face-down dominoes. Match the dots in a straight row to make it easier or attach the dominoes in different directions if it does not confuse the child. Be sure to line up the dots accurately. You can attach a match at either end. The first player to use up her dominoes wins. Because this game may be confusing at first, you can help and re-explain the directions in a way that will help your child understand the concept. You can also just take turns matching the dot configurations from a group of face-down dominoes without setting aside the original five for each player.

MEMORY GAME

Objective

To give the child the opportunity to develop her memory while learning to play an interesting game.

About the Game

You can purchase at most toy stores a game called *Memory* by Milton Bradley. It follows the same principle as the well-known game of *Concentration*. It has 108 cards for matching that can be punched out and stored in an enclosed plastic tray. When the children are experienced with this game, they like to use all the pieces for play, but in the beginning you can use the enclosed storage tray to set up a game for six matches. After that you can gradually increase the number of game pieces you use. You can also make your own memory game by making sets of cards that match from stickers, drawings, letters, numbers, words, shapes, etc.

How to Play

Find pairs and place as many as you think are appropriate on the playing table. Place the cards face down in a random order. The child picks a card and turns it face up on the table. She then picks another one and turns it face up on the table to see if it matches. If the two cards match, she keeps the pair in her match pile. If they do not, she turns them both back over in their original positions, and then you take your turn. You both try to remember which cards were turned over and where they are for your future turns.

MR. MIGHTY MIND

Objective

To give your child the opportunity to develop spatial relations and puzzle ability while learning to play a game.

About the Game

You can purchase *Mr. Mighty Mind* by Leisure Learning at most specialty educational toy stores. It has a series of 5'' × 8'' cards with puzzle outlines on them in ascending order of difficulty. There is a whole set of wooden shape pieces in different colors that are used for placing correctly on the puzzle outline.

How to Play

You take the pieces you need for the puzzle card you are doing. They are indicated on each card. Then try to place them properly on the puzzle part of the card. After you complete card number 1, ask your child to do it. After your child completes card number 1, you do card number 2. Take turns until the cards become too difficult for your child. If your child prefers, she can do all the cards by herself.

A similar game produced by the same company is *Little Planner*. It has the same idea of matching shapes to make larger designs. It contains several variations of increasing difficulty, and it can be played by your child alone, by you two together, or with small groups.

BOARD GAMES

Objective

To give your child the opportunity to practice moving around a board from a start to a finish location and to practice counting while learning to play a competitive game.

About the Game

You can purchase at most toy stores some inexpensive beginning games that are easy to play. *Candyland* and *Chutes and Ladders* by Milton Bradley are the most popular ones. However, there are many other simple ones that you might find as well. You can even make up your own boards with spaces and use large buttons, paper clips, or something similar as the pieces. A good way to make boards is in the shape of letters with arrows to show that you move on them in the direction you learn to write them. (See the illustration.) You can also make a different letter card for each player so that each one cannot see while she is playing if she is winning or losing.

How to Play
Place your playing piece on the *Start* square. Take turns rolling a die or using a spinner from another game. Move your playing piece the appropriate number of spaces. When you land on a dot, you move to the next dot. Continue playing until the first player reaches *End*.

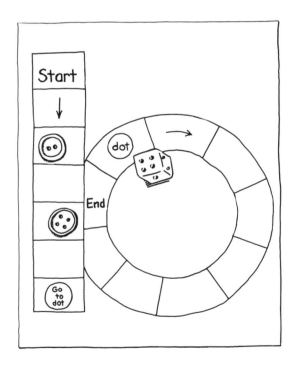

BINGO

Objective
To give your child the opportunity to practice letter and number recognition and beginning graph reading as game-playing skills.

About the Game
You can purchase at most toy stores an inexpensive basic bingo game. In addition, there are many variations that are appealing to children.

How to Play
Place the calling numbers in the specially designed box if there is one. Then give out a board card and a group of markers to each player. Each player places a marker on the free space on her card. The caller calls out a number by its identifying letter as well and places it on a master chart so that it can be referred to again when a player says "Bingo." Any player who has that number on her card places a marker on the corresponding square. The first one to have a row of markers in any direction, across, up and down, or diagonal, is the winner and calls out "Bingo."

DOTS

Objective
To give the child the opportunity to practice drawing straight lines, practice writing her initials, and learn beginning strategy while learning to play a competitive game.

About the Game
The grid can have as few as nine dots or as many as 36. You lay them out on the paper in rows (see illustration). For a younger child you can focus on just making squares, while for an older

child you can introduce the element of trying to keep your opponent from making them.

How to Play
With a pencil, pen, crayon, or marker, set up the grid. Explain to the child the rules. By drawing one line at a time from a dot to a dot, you try to be the one to complete a square. You take turns drawing lines and try not to set it up for the next player to complete a square. Once you complete a square, you put your initial in it and draw another line. The one who has the most squares with her initials in them by the time all dots have been connected by lines is the winner.

Nine dot grid	1st player	2d player	1st player	etc.

Sixteen dot grid

Twenty-five dot grid

Thirty-six dot grid

CARDS

Objective
To give the child the opportunity with a single deck of cards to learn many different concepts and also to enjoy games.

About the Game
Because a set of playing cards has so many different aspects to it—colors, suits, numbers, and pictures—you can make up whatever game will interest your child. Simple sorting by colors or suits is a good starter. If appropriate, teach her at the proper level any simple games you know. You can then go on to play a version of *War* which teaches a lot about number values.

How to Play
In *War* you each have half the deck. From your own cards, you each turn a card over at the same time. The higher card wins the trick and the player with that card keeps both cards. If the two are the same, you have a war. That means you each place three cards down and then one up. The winner this time takes all the cards played. If it is a tie again, you have a war again. You continue in this manner until one player has a higher card showing. The winner of the game is the one who has either all the cards or the most cards when you are ready to stop.

7

Games for Mathematics Development

Preparing children to be as comfortable with the world of numbers and mathematics as they are with the world of letters and reading is important. With the advent of our computer-based society, this becomes even more important than before. Counting, copying, and writing numbers directly are foundation mathematics skills that lead to the formation of the concepts of adding and subtracting. Adding and subtracting can then lead to the ability to multiply and divide, and those skills are the precursors of higher mathematics.

To understand number concepts, children must understand that numbers denote a measurement of magnitude (how big), or distance (how far), or quantity (how many). These ideas all relate to the ability to perceive size. They also have to grasp the idea that numbers have stable values and maintain stable relationships. They are always either smaller or bigger than other numbers and by the same amounts.

TEN LITTLE INDIANS

Objective
To give your child the opportunity to gain a concept of number and number value while singing a song.

About the Game
Using poster board or a large piece of construction paper, make a number chart like the one in the illustration. If you have stickers or pictures of any kinds of Indians, use them in a group of ten on the chart as well. If you have any sets of ten toy little Indians, use them for counting in this activity. There is a set called *Scribblers Bag of Numbers* sold in most educational specialty stores that is helpful in making these charts. It has colorful die-cut numbers and shapes that punch out easily and can be pasted down. Gummed labels in different colors and shapes from a stationery story are also good for making groupings of ten.

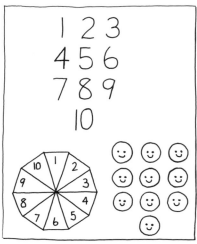

front

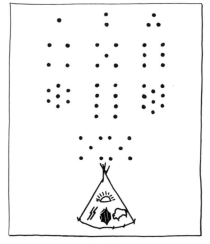

back

How to Play
Each time you sing "The Ten Little Indians," point to one of
the groupings and count each item in the group as you say
each number. Here are the words:

> 1 little, 2 little, 3 little Indians,
> 4 little, 5 little, 6 little Indians,
> 7 little, 8 little, 9 little Indians,
> 10 little Indian boys and girls.

You can also change the word *Indians* to numbers, dots,
triangles, or whatever you are counting. Traditionally this
song has been used for counting our ten fingers. When you do
that, notice what a good finger exercise it is as each finger is
raised one at a time.

FIND THE NUMBER

Objective
To give the child the opportunity to practice counting and to
see how numbers are related to each other by teaching their
relationship spatially.

About the Game
By playing a manipulative game, your child will see that any
particular number is always in the same position on the number line.

How to Play
Use two sets of *Sort O'Cards* numbered from one to ten from
Teaching with Toys, or number two sets of index cards with
large clear numerals from one to ten. Place the corresponding
number of dots on the back. Lay one set of the cards on the
table number side up in ascending order. Mix up the second
set of cards and place them in a pile number side up.

Have your child draw the first card and say the number on it. Tell him to find the match on the number line of cards and to place it on top of the match. Take your turn and continue to play until all the cards from the pile have been matched correctly. A more advanced version of the game would be to match the dot sides of the cards to the number line of cards. In addition, you could use the number side of the cards to match to a dot side number line. You can also use more of the *Sort O' Cards* or numbered index cards and continue the game with cards up to twenty.

THE COUNTING GAME

Objective
To give the child the opportunity to see how numbers are related to each other by teaching their relationship spatially.

About the Game
By playing a manipulative game, the child will see that any particular number is always smaller or bigger than other numbers, and by the same amount. Moreover, by saying equations are part of the game, you are introducing the concept of addition.

How to Play
Use two sets of *Sort O' Cards* numbered from one to ten, from *Teaching with Toys*, or number two sets of index cards with large clear numerals from one to ten. Also make two zero cards with no dots on the back. Lay one set of the cards on the table in a row with the numbers showing in ascending order from zero to ten. Use two small objects like paper clips to be your playing pieces. Place them on the zero card. Use the second set of *Sort O' Cards* or numbered index cards to be the picking cards. Mix them up and place in a pile. Have your

child draw the first card. Tell him to count the cards as he moves his playing piece to reach the numbered card that matches the number on the card he had drawn from the pile. Take your turn and continue playing until one of the players lands his playing piece on the ten. After each move say the equation that represents the move. For example, if four is picked first, the equation is "zero plus four equals four." If two is picked next, you say "four plus two equals six." For a child who would appreciate it, write it out as well. In the beginning, talk and write about equations only up to five. Later, include the ones up to ten as well. When finished with your move, place the card you picked for your turn on the bottom of the pile of cards.

If the card you pick would move past the number ten card, choose the next card to be able to continue to play. You can repeat the game several times. For a more advanced version, you can play the same game by using the dots side of the cards or mix it up using some dots and some numbers. You can also use more of the *Sort O' Cards* or index cards and continue the game with cards up to twenty.

COUNTING BACKWARD

Objective
To give the child the opportunity to practice counting and to see how numbers are related to each other by teaching their relationship spatially.

About the Game
By playing a manipulative game, the child will see that any particular number is always smaller or larger than other numbers, and by the same amounts. This is almost like the *Counting Game*, but it introduces the concept of subtraction. It is set up exactly like the *Counting Game* (described just before

this one), with two sets of cards and a playing piece for each player.

How to Play
Just as in the *Counting Game*, you move your player to the number line card corresponding to the number of the card you picked from the pile. The difference is that once you are on a spot, ask the child, or yourself when it is your turn, to go backward to any number equivalent to or less than the first number. After each move backward, say the equation that represents the move. For example, if four is picked first and you then ask the child to go back to two, the equation is "four minus two equals two." For a child who would appreciate it, write it out as well. In the beginning talk and write about equations only up to five. Later, include ones up to ten as well. After each step backward, place the playing piece on the zero again to get ready for his next turn. The first player to pick card ten is the winner. For that number, do not go backward. You can repeat the game several times. Always play this game after playing the *Counting Game* first.

COPYING EQUATIONS

Objective
To give the child the opportunity to become familiar with the way an equation looks in its written form.

About the Game
Use equations that are at the appropriate level for the child. You will know this from the kind of work, if any, he is doing in school. In addition to gaining familiarity with equations, the child will be getting practice recognizing numbers presented in a new way, reading the left to right progression of numbers, and writing numbers in order.

How to Play
Fold a paper in quarters. In each of the two left-hand spaces, write a simple equation. For example, "2 + 1 = 3" and "4 + 0 = 4." Ask the child to copy the equations in the corresponding right-hand spaces. Once the child can easily write equations horizontally, play the same game with numbers in a vertical position. For example:

$$
\begin{array}{r}
2 \\
+\ 1 \\
\hline
3
\end{array}
\qquad\qquad
\begin{array}{r}
4 \\
+\ 0 \\
\hline
4
\end{array}
$$

EQUATIONS

Objective
To give the child the opportunity to become familiar with doing equations.

About the Game
Use equations that are at the appropriate level for the child. One way to decide is to use the child's age itself. For a three-year-old, you might want to use all the ways to make three. For a four-year-old, use four; for a five-year-old, use five; and for a six-year-old, six. You can use harder equations if appropriate for your child.

How to Play
Fold a paper in quarters. Write the equations that are appropriate for your child on index cards placing the answers on the back. Have the child pick a card one at a time and write the equations with answers in each of the four spaces on the paper. He should try to find the answer without looking at the answer on the back of the card. For whatever number you are using, have small objects like blocks, buttons, or paper clips for the child to manipulate to help him figure out the answer.

After you are finished with the equations cards, you can take them and hide them in different places around the house. Tell your child to say the whole equation each time he finds a card. He can look for them right away or wait and just say them as he comes across them any time.

For another version, again use paper folded in quarters. Use the blocks or other small objects to design the equations. If you are using a group of four blocks, ask the child to separate them into two groups and then say the equation (see illustration). Then have the child write the equation in the spaces on the paper.

Another way to do it would be to lay out the blocks in front of the child and ask him to take one or a few or all away and then say the equation. For example: if you have a group of four and he takes one away, he should say, "four minus one equals three."

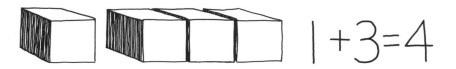

NUMBER CONTAINERS

Objective
To give the child the opportunity to learn number concepts by a manipulative activity and to develop fine motor coordination at the same time.

About the Game
Any eleven plastic containers, cans, or paper or plastic cups will be good for this game. Any eleven labels or small pieces of paper with the numbers marked on them attached to the containers will be good for numbering. It is best to have all the containers and all the labels the same size. Any fifty-five or

more small objects like blocks, paper clips, buttons, etc. will be good for counting.

How to Play
Number the labels from zero to ten and attach them to the containers. Start the game with the containers in order from zero to ten and later use them in any order. Choose container one and ask the child to put the correct number of blocks in it. Then go on to container two and so on up to ten. At the end talk about the zero container and explain why it is empty. When this matching activity becomes easy, mix up the order of the containers.

MONEY CONTAINERS

Objective
To give the child the opportunity to learn money concepts by a manipulative activity and to develop fine motor coordination at the same time.

About the Game
Any five plastic containers with lids or paper or plastic cups upside down will be good for this activity. Any five labels or small pieces of paper with money values and coin names marked on them attached to the containers will be good for the labeling. A large amount of small change—quarters, dimes, nickels, pennies, two to five or more of each coin, and any fifty-cent pieces if you have them—will be needed.

How to Play
Cut small coin-size slits in the lids of the containers or in the bottom of the upside-down cups. Take turns picking a coin from a group on the table and placing it in the container or cup marked with the proper name and value of the coin. For example, a dime should go in the one marked "dime 10¢." As

your child picks each coin, direct him to use his thumb and forefinger only. In this way he will be practicing his pincer grasp as well. As he and you place each coin, you say the coin name and value aloud. When he becomes experienced at this game, have your child say the coin name and value.

For a more advanced version of the activity, ask the child to say the value of two or more coins placed in the same container or cup. Still later, you can fill the containers or cups with the proper coins. Then ask your child to choose two or more coins from different containers and try to tell you the value.

MONEY ON THE SPOT

Objective
To give the child the opportunity to learn money concepts by a manipulative activity and to develop fine motor coordination at the same time.

About the Game
Use five index cards of any size. Make large letters and numbers when you print on the cards. Have a group of coins with all the five values—penny, nickel, dime, quarter, half dollar—ready for play. Only one of each coin is needed for this game.

How to Play
Trace one coin on an index card on both sides. Then print on one side the correct coin name—penny, nickel, dime, quarter, or half dollar—and on the opposite side print the corresponding coin value—1¢, 5¢, 10¢, 25¢, or 50¢. Do this for each of the five on different cards, one per card. Lay the five cards out in a row with the word side up. Then take turns picking from the pile of coins, again with the proper pincer grasp. As you pick a coin, place it in the circle on the proper

card. Every time you place a coin say or have the child say what is written on the card. Keep playing until all the coins have been played. Then return the coins to the original pile and turn over the cards so that the coin values show. Play the game in the same way with the other sides of the cards.

MATH IN A FLASH

Objective
To give the child the opportunity to practice whatever number facts he is learning while playing a game.

About the Game
Prepare the flash cards yourself on any size index cards or use a set of store-bought flash cards. As long as the answers are on the opposite sides of the cards from the equation, they will be fine. A fun way to start play is to make equations for the age of the child. For example, use all the ways to make three:

$0 + 3 =, 1 + 2 =, 2 + 1 =,$ and $3 + 0 =.$

How to Play
Place all the cards in a pile. Draw the top one. Show it to the child. Tell him to try to say the answer before you show the answer on the other side. In the beginning go slowly. As you play and as he gets to know the number facts better, increase your speed.

As in the game *Equations* on pages 93–94, you can take the cards after you have finished and hide them in different places around the house. Your child can look for them right away or just find them as he comes across them. Tell him to say the whole equation each time he finds a card.

PUZZLE MATH

Objective
To give your child the opportunity to practice equations, both addition and subtraction, while playing a puzzle game.

About the Game
You can purchase the *Puzzle Math* game by Leisure Learning at most specialty educational toy stores. It has four board cards with numbers on them and a set of ten puzzle cards for each board with numbers on the back. It also has two dice with numbers and corresponding dots on them.

How to Play
Each person takes a board card and the corresponding ten puzzle cards. Each board card has ten numbered spaces that can be covered by ten numbered puzzle cards. Each puzzle card has a number on one side and a picture on the other. You then take turns rolling the dice. After you roll, add the value of the two dice together. If it makes a number still open on your board card, you match it, number side first, and then turn the card over to its picture side. The object is similar to filling up a card in bingo and lotto games, but because the pictures fit together to make a puzzle, it has the added interest of seeing a puzzle completed. If after adding the two dice on your turn, it doesn't make a number still open on your board card, try subtracting the smaller number from the larger one. If it still does not make a number you need, the next player goes. If the two numbers rolled are the same, subtracting is not an alternative because there is no zero space on the board cards. You can explain that too when the situation comes up.

THE LITTLE PROFESSOR

Objective
To give the child the opportunity to practice math facts while playing a computer game.

About the Game

Little Professor by Texas Instruments is a toy that can be purchased. Other companies make similar toys. If you have access to a home computer and a similar program, that would be fine too. Whatever machine or software you have that practices math facts with children is useful.

How to Play

Set the *Little Professor* or set up a comparable beginning mathematics software program. If using the *Little Professor*, it works like this. Press "ON" to turn on the machine. Press "SET" to set the level and press "LEVEL" until it says "Level 1." Press "GO" to get the first equation. It will say something like "3 + 2." Press your answer. If you press 5, it will automatically show a new equation. If you press a different number, it will show EEE. If you press three wrong numbers in a row, it will automatically show you the correct answer. Press "GO" again to see a new equation. On this computer, a new equation is the reinforcement for being right, and EEE is the response for being wrong. Different software for home computers have different signals for correct and incorrect responses, but the idea of mathematics practice in this way is similar. For a more advanced version on the *Little Professor*, set it at level 2. Levels 3 and 4 are quite advanced.

A more advanced computer toy is *Speak and Math* also by Texas Instruments. It has a voice that both reads the equation and also says whether the answer is correct or not. The toy also has four levels of difficulty for the equations and for other types of mathematics activities. There are other modules, program discs, available for this toy for different levels of mathematics skill. Because the skill levels get quite advanced, even with the basic module, it is a toy your child will get use out of for a long time.

8

Games for Gross Motor Development

One of the best things you can do for a young growing child is to take her to a playground. Besides the play time and physical exercise time you know you are providing, you are actually giving your child the opportunity to grow in other ways as well.

Each piece of equipment moves or helps a child move through space in a way important for proper developmental growth. Swings move the child back and forth, merry-go-rounds around, slides up and down, and jungle gyms in all directions. Many playgrounds have large sand areas for tactile stimulation as well as fine motor and creativity development. The movement available in this environment provides stimulation to a growing brain. The brain growth slows down at about six years old and is finished at about eight years of age. The brain continues to learn forever but never again as well as it did when it was still growing. It grows the fastest and learns the most from birth and keeps slowing down after that.

In addition, there are many movement activities you can do at home, some inside and some outside. Some are sports and some lay the foundation for later sports. Some build eye-hand coordination and others refine general body co-ordination. All develop concentration so valuable to success at any endeavor.

BIKE RIDING

Objective
To give your child the opportunity to practice a cross pattern-ing body movement while receiving both exercise and de-velopmental stimulation.

About the Game
A bicycle, with training wheels or without, depending on the age and ability of your child, is appropriate. At whatever level, the child should be encouraged to develop her skills.

How to Play
Take out the bicycle and watch your child ride it. If she needs help in any way, provide it. If not, watch her ride and let her know you are enjoying her fun too. A variation for at home is to do the bicycle exercise with her feet. As she lies on the floor opposite you, move her feet in a bicycle motion to help her with the pattern. As you hold her legs under her knees, keep your hands in the position they would be in if you were holding handlebars. You can sing "Bicycle Built for Two" as you pedal her feet if you wish.

Teaching a child to ride a two-wheeler is a little like teaching some of the other childhood milestones like walk-ing, skipping, even toilet training and reading. Every parent reports a slightly different method, and no one method seems to work for all children. Some children after seeing older children ride can get on a two-wheeler and ride too. Others need training-wheel practice for a long time, and others need long hours of someone running with them as they then main-tain their own balance for longer and longer periods of time. No two children are alike, but all should be encouraged to perfect this skill. It will give them many hours of fun, inde-pendence, and positive developmental training.

ROLLER-SKATING

Objective
To give your child the opportunity to practice cross pattern-ing body movement and balance while receiving both exer-cise and developmental stimulation.

About the Game
Experience on skates is the important part. For how long and at what level of activity depends on the age and ability of the child. Fisher-Price makes a roller skate that is adjustable in size and fits over the shoe that can be set at first to not roll backward. It can later be changed to roll in both directions. These and other over-the-shoe skates are available in most toy stores. Shoe skates can be found in most toy, sporting goods, and department stores.

How to Play
Teach your child at the appropriate level how to put on and take off her skates. For a beginner teach her to walk in her skates. As she progresses, encourage her to take longer strides. Always stress using arms for balance. If ice-skating is more accessible in your location, teach that instead of or in addition to roller-skating.

MOVEMENT IN SPACE

Objective
To give your child the opportunity to practice directing her own body and to develop muscle strength while receiving both exercise and developmental stimulation.

About the Game
You can use a skateboard or a homemade version. If you

make one, use a small piece of wood about 12″ × 18″ × 1″ and put on four ball bearing casters, one in each corner. Be sure to sand the corners well. You can get the casters in most hardware or home supply stores.

Another play item available in most toy stores is *Sit 'n' Spin*. The child sits on it and through manipulation of her hands and arms turns her body. Spinning is another body movement that is good for a child's development.

How to Play
Tell your child she is going to operate her new vehicle. You can call it her car if that would make it more fun. She can sit on it or lie on it on her tummy. Any way she or you choose, she is the operator and must use her arm and leg muscles to move herself about.

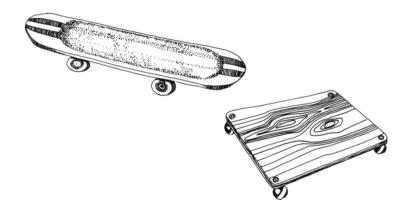

EXERCISES

Objective
To give your child the opportunity to do basic exercises that will improve her stamina, develop muscles in all parts of her body, and provide for developmental stimulation.

About the Game

Choose exercises that will move muscles in different parts of the body. You can also use the record *Sesame Street Exercise* by Children's Television Workshop as a guide or for following along with the record.

How to Play

You become the exercise class leader, and have your child or children follow. You can all wear leotards if you have them or appropriate gymnastics outfits for boys. Be enthusiastic. Make it fun. Some suggested exercises are:

1. Jack be nimble. Place on the ground a small object or card over which she can jump and learn to jump farther and better each time.
2. Walk on construction paper circles. Increase the distance gradually each time. Tape them to the floor so they will not slip.
3. Walk balancing a bean bag on your head.
4. Walk on a line (masking tape or drawn with chalk outside), on a piece of plywood (about 4 inches wide), or a 2 × 4 (laid flat on the floor) about 8 feet long.
5. Get up from the floor without touching your arms to the floor.
6. Hold your child's legs and walk her like a wheelbarrow on her arms.
7. Bend down and walk like a duck.
8. Skipping. Show it slowly as step-hop on each leg.
9. Hopping.
10. Galloping. First slide to the left and then slide to the right.
11. Crab walk. From a sitting position, walk on all fours, feet and hands and not knees and hands, because your back is facing the floor, not your stomach.
12. Seal walk. From lying on your tummy, drag your feet and walk with your arms.

13. Bridge. From a lying down position on your back raise yourself up on your hands with your hands facing backwards.
14. Somersaults.
15. Ballet or other dances. Practice any steps you or your child know.

USING A LARGE BALL

Objective
To give your child the opportunity to develop eye-hand co-ordination in a way that will lay the foundation for later ball-playing activities.

About the Game
Use a ball that is 12″ to 18″ in diameter. Rolling the ball back and forth is the first level of ball play. Beach balls are good for this activity because they are soft, safe, and inexpensive. You must watch the ball as it rolls to you from the person who rolled it, and you must look at the person to whom you are rolling it to direct it to that person. Catch is the next level. You play this standing up and use the same eye movements. If you have a large enough area away from breakables, you can play indoors. Kickball adds more dimension but that must be played outdoors. You first learn to roll the ball to someone who is kicking. As kicker you learn to kick the ball. Depending on the age of the child, you can teach some beginning rules about the bases.

How to Play
Choose one or more of the activities described depending on your child's interest. You start with the ball and explain what to do as you demonstrate. If it is rolling the ball, explain the idea of following the ball when it comes to you and looking at the person when you are rolling it. If it is catch, explain and demonstrate the same principles. If it is kickball, explain the rules. Be enthusiastic, share in the fun, and play together.

BAT AND BALL

Objective
To give your child the opportunity to develop eye-hand co-ordination in a way that will lay the foundation for learning to play baseball.

About the Game
Use a plastic bat and ball. Balls with holes in them called whiffle balls are excellent. Set up some kind of home plate, even a paper plate, and direct your child to stand sideways next to it. Show her the correct way to hold a bat and the correct way to swing. This can be only an outdoor activity.

How to Play
Pitch the ball slowly and as close to the bat as possible. Be patient and encouraging and keep reminding her to watch the ball. This is a difficult skill. After you have practiced her batting, switch to a game of catch with the baseball. Show her the correct position for her feet for throwing overhand correctly. Throw it back to her in an easy underhand style.

SPONGE BALL THROUGH A HOLE

Objective
To give the child the opportunity to develop eye-hand coordination while playing a game.

About the Game
Use an old towel or part of an old sheet. Cut a hole in the center of it, any size, as long as it is larger than the sponge ball. If you don't have a sponge ball, sometimes called a Nerf ball, use a soft sponge.

How to Play
Hold the piece of fabric with hole cut in the middle out to your side. Ask the child to throw the sponge ball through the hole. If she misses, she can pick it up and try again. If she gets it through, change the position of the piece of fabric. You can also take turns throwing the ball and holding the cloth.

BOWLING

Objective
To give the child the opportunity to develop eye-hand coordination while playing a game.

About the Game
In most toy stores there are inexpensive plastic bowling sets that you can purchase. You can also make your own set of pins and a ball. A good size and weight for the pins are empty potato chip cans. A good ball is any small one you have, or you can use a filled can about soup can size instead of a ball.

How to Play
Set up the pins in the same grouping as on a real bowling alley—a row of four, a row of three in front of it, a row of two

in front of that, and one pin in the front. Put the game out on a patio, in a playroom, or in any other open area. It should also have enough room for rolling the ball or can toward the pins. Teach as many of the rules of real bowling as is appropriate for the age and interest of your child. Explain the setup of the pins and how the formation equals ten. Take turns with your child and share in the fun.

GOLF

Objective
To give your child the opportunity to develop eye-hand co-ordination while playing a game.

About the Game
In most toy stores there are inexpensive children's golf sets that you can purchase, some plastic and other more expensive metal ones. I recommend a set of plastic clubs called *Hole in One* by Mattel that have clubs with wide heads on them for hitting the ball, a large plastic golf ball, and a specially designed cup.

How to Play
Set up the cup on the lawn or on a low pile carpeted area. A floor is usually too slippery to keep the ball still before hitting it. Place the ball seven or eight feet away or whatever distance you feel is appropriate for your child. Show your child how to properly hold the club and how to stand sideways to the ball so that she will have the most success getting the ball into the cup. Take turns with your child and share in the fun. A word of caution, it is not so easy.

TENNIS

Objective
To give your child the opportunity to develop eye-hand co-ordination while playing a game.

About the Game
A racquetball racquet is a good size and weight to use to teach your child beginning tennis. In most toy stores there are also inexpensive plastic paddle sets that come with a sponge ball.

How to Play
Show your child how to hold the racquet. (See the photograph.) At different ages because of varying strength, children will be holding it in different ways. Strive for as close to proper form as possible and focus on telling your child to watch the ball.

HIDE-AND-SEEK

Objective
To give your child the opportunity to develop an awareness of her body in space by playing a game.

About the Game
This is an age-old game passed on from generation to generation that has a lot of educational aspects to it. To hide, you have to figure out a place in which your body will fit. Counting practice from one to ten or twenty is also part of the game, and running to hide is good exercise.

How to Play
Tell your child you will count to ten or twenty and that she should go and hide. After you have counted, explain that you will try to find her. After you find her, you can start all over again; or she can count and then try to find you after you hide.

9

Games for Fine Motor Development

There are three major areas of muscles that need to be worked for fine motor development—fingers and the hand as they manipulate objects, the forefinger and thumb as they work together in a pincer grasp, and the wrist. Throughout the child's day, he faces many opportunities to exercise in all those areas. In addition, there are other activities that are fun and can be added to his everyday experiences. Because there are so many ways to play and work in these areas, this chapter is divided into three parts: Manipulative, Pincer, and Wrist. All the movements will contribute to the specific skills of writing and drawing and the general achievement of eye-hand coordination.

Gross motor development is basic to fine motor development. The principle is similar to that of a tree's growth. The trunk and root system must be healthy and strong for the branches, stems, and leaves to thrive. Therefore, general body exercise should be kept up along with all the fine motor experiences.

Manipulative

PLAY DOUGH AND CLAY

Objective
To give your child the opportunity to develop manipulative skills while expanding his creativity.

About the Game
There is a progression of play dough and clay activities that may be followed when this medium is introduced—touching and feeling it for familiarity, rolling into a ball, patting the ball into a pancake, making the pancake into a happy face, and then rolling out the pancake into coils for building into pottery type figures. This whole series provides stimulation for all the muscles in the fingers and hands. Whether you are using store-bought play dough or homemade, be sure to store it in plastic containers with lids so that it will not dry out.

   If you are using clay, choose a plasticine that can be left uncovered and still not dry out. Most toy stores or five-and-tens carry it. There is also a set called *The Little Sculptor* by Creative Playthings that comes with an excellent quality clay and a set of plastic sculptor's tools that are also good for developing manipulative skills.

How to Play
Each of you take a piece of play dough or clay the same size. You demonstrate the project with your piece and ask him to try to make what you are making. Go through the progression listed above. From those basics you can make many things—snowmen, people with arms and legs, snakes, dishes, animals, etc. You can also make letters out of the coils. It is often fun to make a letter and cover it up with a washcloth. Ask him to feel under the cloth and try to figure out what letter it is. He can also make a letter, hide it under a cloth, and have you guess it by feeling. This activity helps to develop the sense of touch.

SEWING

Objective
To give your child the opportunity to develop manipulative skills while expanding his creativity.

About the Game
There are several possibilities for a successful sewing experience for your child. In most toy stores there are inexpensive lacing or sewing card sets. In addition, there are home versions that are just as interesting, if not more. If making a card, use a small piece of construction paper or poster board, even a 5″ × 8″ index card, hole punched where you would like the child to sew. The holes can be around a flower design, in the letters of your child's name, around the outer rim, or in some other picture. Take a piece of yarn and tie a knot on the end of it. Then put some tape around the sewing tip of it to make a firm end like the end of a shoelace. If the holes are big enough, you could use shoelaces instead of yarn.

How to Play
Teach your child to put the yarn up through the hole from the back and down through the hole from the front. If doing a border, you can show him how to come up from the bottom

each time. In the beginning the yarn might twist a lot so help your child as he pulls the yarn through.

Another interesting idea is to take a plastic basket, the kind fresh produce sometimes comes in, and a longer piece of yarn. Use tape to make a point on the yarn and tie the other end to one slat of the basket. Show your child how to weave the yarn in and out.

The next level is using a blunt darning or needlepoint needle and yarn on a small piece of needlepoint material, plastic, canvas, or other loosely knit fabric about eight inches square. In the beginning children will enjoy sewing just for the fun of sewing without making anything you can recognize. Later they will become interested in making specific designs. Before long with your guidance they will be able to make their own simple pouches and potholders. Still later you will be able to help them make basic doll clothes or even sew netting into ballet skirts.

If your child has the interest after mastering beginning sewing, you might even want to start him on beginning knitting using large wooden needles. If you do not have yarn available, string will work well. It knots less and is easier to manipulate.

WHERE IS THUMBKIN?

Objective
To give your child the opportunity to develop manipulative skills while singing a song.

About the Game
This is an age-old children's song passed down from generation to generation that provides finger exercises. The more practice the child has with this song, the better he will be able to do the finger movements.

How to Play

Sit opposite your child and do the singing and motions of the song together. Help him as much as is necessary to do the proper finger movements on each hand. Here are the words and the corresponding finger motions.

Words	*Actions*
Where is thumbkin?	Hold up left thumb.
Where is thumbkin?	Hold up right thumb.
Here I am.	Move left thumb.
Here I am.	Move right thumb.
How are you today, sir?	Move left thumb.
Very well I thank you.	Move right thumb.
Run away.	Move left hand behind back.
Run away.	Move right hand behind back.

Repeat the verse four more times, substituting a different finger each time. The index finger is traditionally called "pointer"; the middle finger, "tall man"; the ring finger, "ringman"; and the small outside finger, "pinky."

WHEELS ON THE BUS

Objective

To give your child the opportunity to develop hand, arm, and body coordination while singing a song.

About the Game

This is an age-old children's song passed down from generation to generation that provides exercises for hand, arm, and body coordination. The more practice the child has with this song, the better he will be able to do the movements.

How to Play

Sit opposite your child and do the singing and motions of the song together. Help him as much as is necessary to do the proper movements. Here are the words and their corresponding motions.

Words	*Actions*
The wheels on the bus go round and round, round and round, round and round. The wheels on the bus go round and round, all through the town.	Cross your arms across your chest and move them in a parallel position around and around each other.
The doors on the bus go open and shut, open and shut, open and shut. The doors on the bus go open and shut, all through the town.	Open your arms wide and bring them together by having your hands meet in the middle of your body.

Other Verses

The wipers on the bus go swish, swish, swish.	Move your hands at the wrists from side to side.
The people on the bus go up and down.	Raise your child up and down or stand up and sit down with him.
The babies on the bus go wah, wah, wah.	Pretend to be crying and wiping your eyes.
The mommies on the bus go sh, sh, sh.	Cover your mouth with your forefinger as you say, "sh."
The daddies on the bus go hm, hm, hm.	Put your hands on your waist as you say, "hm."
(Others of your own choice)	Act out the words.

MAKING DOLL CLOTHES WITHOUT SEWING

Objective
To give your child the opportunity to develop manipulative skills while creating.

About the Game
This activity provides practice with a scissors, tying if the child is ready, and the handling of a doll and its outfits. In addition, it develops creativity by giving the child the opportunity to design and choose outfits for a doll.

How to Play
Cut rectangles of fabric the appropriate size for your child's doll. Use large ones for dresses and smaller ones for blouses. In each case have your child cut a hole in it for the head. Then show how to tie a ribbon sash on it to make it fit. For skirts, show how to wrap a rectangle and secure it with a ribbon.

HOMEMADE PUZZLES

Objective
To give your child the opportunity to develop manipulative skills by making and then using his own homemade puzzle.

About the Game
There are many sources of interesting pictures for homemade puzzles. You can cut the puzzle pieces to be easy to put together or more difficult.

How to Play
Select interesting magazine pages (*Sesame Street Magazine* is a good source), paper place mats from restaurants, simple colorful maps, or a picture your child has colored. Show him how to apply paste to one side and then paste it onto a piece of

cardboard the same size as the picture. Have him draw lines on the back for puzzle pieces. Cut along those lines to make the pieces. You can help your child with this part as much or as little as is needed. Then work with your child on putting the puzzle back together. If you used a map, talk about the directions with your child. If appropriate, see if he can figure out a route from one place to another.

It is also a good idea to work with your child on store-bought puzzles of increasing difficulty. Start with eight-piece wooden ones and go up to ten, twelve, and fifteen pieces. After he masters one, go on to another. Then there are many inexpensive frame cardboard puzzles with twelve to fifteen pieces. After that there are regular jigsaw puzzles with as few as twenty-five pieces going up in difficulty to as many as a thousand pieces. If you can find a map of the United States, with each state as a piece, use it. Slowly he will become familiar with the fifty states, maybe even their capitals too. First talk about the state you are in and then those you have visited and where relatives live.

STRAW OR PENCIL PASSING

Objective
To give your child the opportunity to develop manipulative skills while playing a game.

About the Game
Regular drinking straws work best for this game. If straws are not available, look for a group of pencils or sticks of uniform diameter, such as those found in Tinkertoys.

How to Play
Give the straws to him one at a time all in one hand so that he will have to manipulate them to hold them. Then take the group back and pass them all to his other hand, one at a time.

You can then ask him to pass them to you one at a time using only the hand he is holding them in, so he will again have to manipulate the straws.

TWISTING AND BRAIDING

Objective
To give your child the opportunity to develop manipulative skills while creating.

About the Game
In the beginning start with twisting. Then go on to braiding when your child is ready.

How to Play
Attach two and then three pieces of thick yarn to a door knob. Show your child how to twist and then braid when he is ready. If you have thin yarn, prepare two or three strands together as one piece. Help him as little or as much as is necessary. If your yarn is long enough, you can tie knots at each end of the braid and show your child how it can be worn as a belt.

PIANO

Objective
To give your child the opportunity to develop manipulative skills by playing music.

About the Game
Use a play piano or real one if you have it. In most toy stores there are many small keyboard toys as well as full child-size pianos.

How to Play

Show the child on the piano where middle C is. If you are not sure, check any information sheets that come with your piano or ask a friend who would know. Tell him to place his thumb on that key and then to play a five-note scale up to G, using each successive finger to press the next key. If it is a large piano, he can then put his thumb on any C and play a five-note scale from there. If you can play the piano and if he shows interest, teach the rest of the scale. If you or he feel it is appropriate, you can then go on to teach other fingerings for simple songs. Often pianos come with instructions to teach beginning skills.

SPINNER

Objective

To give your child the opportunity to develop manipulative skills by playing a game.

About the Game

Look around the house for a spinner from a game. They are often in simple beginning ones. Instead of using the board and playing the game, make up some action you and your child can do the number of times the spinner indicates after you spin it. Jumps, hops, claps, etc. are all fun to do.

How to Play

Show your child the correct way to hold and then spin a spinner. Ask him first to decide on the action and then to spin first. After he takes his turn, take yours. Help him as little or as much as is necessary using the spinner.

BUILDING TOYS

Objective
To give your child the opportunity to develop manipulative skills while using different children's building materials.

About the Game
Any of the building sets available like Lego, blocks, Bristle Blocks, Tinkertoys, Lincoln Logs, etc. are good for this activity. If they come with a booklet showing sample structures, save it. The idea behind this activity is to try to build something that they see. If there is no booklet or if those pictures in the booklet look too difficult, make a simpler structure as a model.

Tangrams, a set of eight pieces cut from a square that can be formed into many different shapes, is another good alternative. A set comes with a booklet showing different pictures you can make. It is available at most specialty educational toy stores.

How to Play
Show the picture or the model to your child. Ask him to try to build one the same. Help as little or as much as is necessary. This kind of activity also helps to develop map-reading skills.

OPEN SHUT THEM

Objective
To give your child the opportunity to develop manipulative skills while singing a song.

About the Game
This is an age-old children's song passed down from generation to generation that provides hand and finger exercises. The more practice the child has with this song, the better he

will be able to do the movements. Here are the words with the accompanying motions.

Words	*Actions*
Open shut them, Open shut them,	Open your hands wide and shut them tight (twice).
Give a little clap, clap, clap.	Clap your hands.
Open shut them, Open shut them,	Open your hands wide and shut them tight (twice).
Put them in your lap, lap, lap.	Put your hands in your lap.

Creep them, creep them,
Slowly creep them,
Right up to your chin, chin,
    chin.
	From your lap, creep your
	    fingers slowly up on your
	    body to your chin.

Open up your little mouth, But do not let them in.	Point to your open mouth. Hide your hands behind your back.

How to Play

Sit opposite your child. In preparation for this song you can do additional hand and finger exercises. For the hands show your child how to open them real wide and then shut them into tight fists. Repeat together a few times. For the fingers show him how to match and then press his fingers together. Start with the two thumbs. Then add the forefingers, then the middle fingers, then the ring finger, and then the pinkies. Show him how to give all five fingers a good press open and then shut both hands tight. Do this matching and pressing together. Now you are ready to sing and do the actions of the song together. Help him as much as is necessary to do the movements.

Pincer

TEARING AND PASTING PAPER

Objective
To give your child the opportunity to develop pincer grasp while creating.

About the Game
Construction paper is good for tearing. White typing paper is good for the background. Simple white glue or paste is easy to apply with the forefinger.

How to Play
Show your child how to tear paper into small pieces with his thumb and forefinger on both hands. When all the tearing is done, draw your child's initials in thick outlines on the white paper. If using glue, show him how to squeeze it on to the area where his initials are outlined. Then show him how to use his forefinger to spread it all over the letters. If using paste, show him how to apply the paste to the area with his initials and then how to spread it over the whole area. An alternative is to put paste on each piece as you apply it, but that is a little more difficult and sometimes more messy. Show him that he is going to fill in all the white spaces of his initials with the torn pieces. You can take turns making this mosaic.

JACKS AND/OR BUTTONS PICKUP

Objective
To give your child the opportunity to develop pincer grasp while playing a game.

About the Game
Put some jacks or a collection of small buttons in a container. You will not be using the ball from the jacks set. Since these are small items that could easily be swallowed, do not leave your child playing this game alone.

How to Play
Empty the jacks or buttons out of the container. Take turns with your child using your thumb and forefinger picking up one at a time and placing it back in the container. You can also use a group of coins in a container. If that is the case, name each coin as you pick it up and say its value. Encourage your child to do the same.

CLOTHESPIN PUPPETS

Objective
To give your child the opportunity to develop pincer grasp while being creative.

About the Game
Use the clothespins, plastic or wooden, that have a metal spring in them. Be sure the spring is attached well so that it will not come off.

How to Play
Give your child one clothespin and show him how to pinch it on one end so that it opens on the other. Show him how to open and close it in such a way that while he talks he can pretend it is a puppet. Give him another for his other hand when he is ready. Take two yourself, and play along with your two clothespin puppets.

TYPEWRITER

Objective
To give your child the opportunity to develop strength in his forefinger while creating.

About the Game
Use a real typewriter, if possible. Play ones often do not work well. An electric is fine but a manual is much better for developing strength. This whole activity should be done under your supervision.

How to Play
Show your child that pressing a key will make that letter or symbol on the paper. Then instruct him to make a whole row of the first letter of his name with his forefinger. Continue with a row of the second letter and so on for all the letters of his name. Whenever appropriate for your child, you can show him how to type his own name. If he is ready and you feel competent, go on to teach any other typing skill.

TELEPHONE

Objective
To give your child the opportunity to develop strength in his forefinger while learning about the telephone.

About the Game
In most toy stores there are inexpensive play telephones. If you are buying one, check to make sure the push buttons or dials are easy to use. A disconnected phone is also good, if available. A real telephone should be used once your child has acquired the basics.

How to Play

Teach your child to press or dial, depending on what kind of phone you have, the first number of your telephone number after you say it. Repeat several times. Then say the first two numbers and have him press those. In this manner go on to three and increase gradually to all the seven numbers. On a real phone, keep the receiver button down until you are ready for all seven numbers. On a real phone, if dialed correctly, you will get a busy signal. It may be hard to explain why to your child, but you can try. After he has mastered your number, try the local time number. With that number someone will always answer and you won't be bothering a friend or neighbor. Do not repeat it too often at one sitting and caution him not to do this activity without your knowledge or supervision.

PEGBOARD PATTERNS

Objective

To give your child the opportunity to develop pincer grasp while playing a game.

About the Game

In most speciality educational toy stores you can find pegs and pegboards of different sizes. If you cannot find them, you can use plastic multicolored toothpicks from any super-market.

How to Play

Across the top of the pegboard place a row of pegs, each a different color, and then repeat the pattern. If you are using colored toothpicks, make a pattern across the top of the surface on which you are working. A flat piece of styrofoam provides a good surface for toothpicks to stand up, but they can also lie flat on a table. Ask your child to take from the group of leftover pegs (or toothpicks) a color that matches the first one and place it under it in a second row. You do the second match. Take turns until the whole row is completed and then start the next row. After all of the pegs (or toothpicks) are used up, you can take them all out and start again with another pattern. A harder variation is to build a pattern on the left side of the board (or surface) and have your child match it on the right. You can take turns building and matching.

BUTTON PRACTICE

Objective
To give your child the opportunity to develop pincer grasp while playing a game.

About the Game
You can use any large piece of clothing that has buttons on it that are of the appropriate size for your child to button and unbutton. A shirt of yours or of an older brother or sister, a jacket, sweater, or robe of his are other possibilities.

How to Play
Help him put the garment on, crossing one arm into the sleeve and then the other. Find a button in the easiest position and ask him to start with that. Take turns buttoning and then unbuttoning the rest of the garment. He can do all the buttons if he wishes. Help as little or as much as is necessary, showing in a slow way how to hold the button as you push it through.

STRINGING MACARONI OR CEREAL

Objective
To give your child the opportunity to develop pincer grasp while creating.

About the Game
Use a piece of yarn, necklace or bracelet size. Put a piece of scotch tape on one end to make the stringing tip and knot the other end. Fill a small container with macaroni or cereal that can be strung.

How to Play
Demonstrate how to put the macaroni or cereal on the yarn and push it down toward the knot. Take turns making the same necklace or bracelet, or each of you make your own. Help as little or as much as is necessary.

ITSY BITSY SPIDER

Objective
To give your child the opportunity to develop muscles in his forefinger and thumb while singing a song.

About the Game
This is an age-old children's song passed down from generation to generation that provides finger exercises. It also has hand and arm movements. The more practice the child has with the song, the better he will be able to do the motions.

Here are the words and their corresponding finger, hand, and arm motions.

Words	*Actions*
The itsy bitsy spider went up the water spout.	Place thumb to forefinger and forefinger to thumb so that they make a rectangular shape. Keep shifting the bottom thumb and forefinger to become the top thumb and forefinger and raise them slightly as you sing.
Down came the rain and washed the spider out.	Wiggle fingers in a downward motion. Stretch out arms to the sides.
Out came the sun and dried up all the rain.	Raise hands over head in a circular position and move from side to side.
And the itsy bitsy spider went up the spout again.	Thumb to forefinger and forefinger to thumb, raising hands as you sing.

How to Play
Sit opposite your child and do the singing and motions of the song together. Help him as much as is necessary to do the proper movements.

LACING A SHOE

Objective
To give your child the opportunity to lace a shoe while playing a game.

About the Game
Choose a shoe for this activity that will be fun. An old baby shoe, or a large shoe from an older brother or sister, mommy, or daddy usually works well.

How to Play

Take the shoelace out of the shoe. Get the lacing started. Then take turns putting the lace through one hole at a time. If that activity goes well, continue to teach tying the shoelace. Help your child as much as he needs it. Break down the activity into small steps for any part that is difficult for the child.

Look for other shoes around the house that close in other ways. Practice any that have buckles. You might even find some boots with interesting fasteners or zippers, or have some fun with any Velcro closings.

Wrist

WINDUP TOYS

Objective
To give your child the opportunity to develop strength in his wrists by playing.

About the Game
You should be able to find whatever you need for this game right in your own home. First collect any windup toys you have like a jack-in-the-box, the Fisher-Price windup record player, any windup children's clock, baby musical toys, even small windup animals and figures. If you do not have any of these, or even if you do, you can use a windup can opener, jars with covers to twist off, a tube of toothpaste (practice twisting the cap off and on), or many other household items.

How to Play
Ask your child to wind up one of the items selected. You take your turn and wind up another one. Give as much or as little help as your child needs. If he wants, he can do all the winding himself.

THE TOSSING GAME

Objective
To give your child the opportunity to develop strength in his wrists by playing.

About the Game
If you have bean bags available for tossing, use a shoe box or another kind of similar size. If you have rings from an old baby toy or some plastic links or blocks, use a round bucket or rectangular wash basin. Bean bags are easy and inexpensive to make. Buy any simple dry beans at the supermarket and use any scraps of fabric that do not fray when cut, like felt. Cut

into double small pieces, sew into a bag, fill with some beans, and sew opening closed.

How to Play

Hold the pile of bean bags or whatever you decide to use and hand them to your child one at a time. Ask him to stand in one central location. Place the container a few feet away from him to his left. Ask him to throw the bean bag into it. If he misses, pick it up and give it back to him for another try. If he gets it in, give him another one for tossing and move the container a few feet around him in a clockwise direction. Continue giving bean bags until the container is moved all the way around to the child's right side. Then take your turn at tossing. Have your child pass you the objects and also move the container around you clockwise after you get them in successfully.

HAMMERING

Objective

To give your child the opportunity to develop strength in his wrists while playing.

About the Game

In most toy stores there are inexpensive hammer and peg sets. Sandberg makes a good one called *Play Tools* on which you bang eight pegs flat on one side and then turn it over and bang them back flat on the other. If you are handy with wood, you could probably make your own version. Besides the wrist strength development, hammering develops eye-hand coordination and is a good outlet for energy.

How to Play
Show your child how to hammer one peg flat. Then give him the hammer to take his turn. He can do all the pegs himself or take turns with you.

POURING

Objective
To give your child the opportunity to develop strength in his wrists by playing.

About the Game
You can use any small pitchers you have in the house, preferably plastic. Measuring cups with pouring spouts work well. You can also use whatever plastic glasses or cups or play cups you have available.

How to Play
Fill with water one of the pitchers or cups you are using. Ask your child to pour out the water into one or more of the other pitchers or cups. Then take your turn pouring. If your child wants to do all the pouring, that is fine. Help as little or as much as is necessary. If your child is interested, you can turn the activity into a real or pretend "tea party." In addition, you can use this opportunity to teach the concept of conservation, explaining that a certain amount of water remains the same whether it is in a short, wide container or in a tall, thin one.

POTATO CARRY

Objective
To give your child the opportunity to develop strength in his wrists while playing.

About the Game
Use a soup spoon and a potato small enough that it will not fall off the spoon easily. If no potatoes are available, use a piece of fruit such as an orange or an apple or another object with some weight to it that is about the size of a potato.

How to Play
Give your child the potato or equivalent object on a soup spoon. Check to see that he can balance it well. Then walk a distance away from him, about six feet at first, and tell him to carry the potato on the spoon back to you. If it is easy for him at this distance, walk farther away the next time. You can do this activity over and over using a greater distance each time. Play a few times in a row and take your turn walking the potato to your child.

LIFTING WEIGHTS

Objective
To give your child the opportunity to develop strength in his wrists while playing.

About the Game
Make a set of half-pound weights for your child by dividing a pound of sugar into two small plastic sandwich bags. You could use beans or sand or other substances, but sugar comes in one-pound packages that can be easily divided. Fasten each bag shut with ties and use three or four bags, one on top of the other with ties, to make sure the sugar doesn't leak. If the

activity becomes easy with half-pound weights, put the two halves together in a brown bag and make a one-pound weight.

How to Play
Show your child how to lift the weight, palm up, into the air. Count five lifts and then ask him to change hands for five more lifts. After he does it, take your turn. Each time you play, increase the number of lifts by two or three. Continue to play for a few rounds until your child has had enough or is ready to go on to the one-pound size.

YO-YO

Objective
To give your child the opportunity to develop strength in his wrists by playing.

About the Game
Most toy stores sell inexpensive yo-yos. The wooden ones are balanced well and work better than the plastic ones. There is also a plastic toy called *Yo-ball* which is even easier to operate.

How to Play
Tie a small ring that will fit easily around your child's finger at the end of the yo-yo string. Show him how to place that ring over his middle finger and balance the yo-yo up and down slowly. Take your turn as well. After learning to operate it up and down in a rhythm, he may be able to learn to make it go out to the side, or to do another advanced trick. Often yo-yos come with instructions.

ZIP

Objective
To give your child the opportunity to develop strength in his wrist by playing a game.

About the Game
You can use any piece of clothing that has a zipper on it large enough that your child will be able to manipulate it. A jacket or sweater from any member of the family is a good source.

How to Play
If it is not too large, your child can wear the selected garment. Show how to hold it firmly as he lifts the tab on the zipper up and down. At first you can hook it in at the bottom for him, but later you can show him how to do that as well. Take turns with him until he has had enough.

SPOONING

Objective
To give your child the opportunity to develop strength in his wrists by playing.

About the Game
For the spooning, you can use any dried peas or beans. If these are not available, find something similar like nuts or raisins. Use a weighted box like one filled with tissues or napkins as a backstop for the spoon because it is hard to scoop up something so small from a flat table surface without using your fingers to help. Use any cup, about measuring cup size, for putting the peas or beans in and a regular shaped teaspoon for picking them up.

How to Play

Take out six or seven peas or beans and put them in front of the weighted box. Put the cup on the side opposite the hand with which the child is holding his spoon. Place the box in front of the child. Ask him to pick up one pea or bean at a time with his spoon and place it in the cup. You can take your turn with the next one or have the child pick them all up by himself.

A variation of this activity is to take a bowl full of beans and ask the child to transfer the beans to an empty bowl by spooning them. It takes less wrist control to scoop a group of beans and transfer them to another location than it does to scoop up only one and transfer it. A child may enjoy this activity after completing the others.

10

The Home Environment

"They will learn what you are and not what you say" is a well-known statement in the field of child development. Our job as parents is like that of a director of children. The end goal is for them to be able to function well on their own, but they need lots of guidance through the years. We must interact with our children and model behavior and be careful not to be constantly correcting and criticizing. The games presented in this book provide a structure for demonstrating a style of leadership. They can be used in the game situation and then also be reminders of how to teach many other ideas that come up from day to day.

"Home is where the heart is" is another well-known statement. Because a home is basically set up for adults, with everything in it of adult size, try to think of all the ways you can modify it so that it is child-size as well. A low coffee table for you can be a regular-size table for a child if used with low stools as chairs. Bulletin boards and pictures in a child's room, usually placed at an adult's eye level, can be lowered. Check around your home to see if you can lower hooks for children to hang their own things on and closet racks for them to hang up their own clothes. For high closet racks you might want to make a sturdy step stool available. Check drawers and shelves to see if they are easy enough for children to manipulate and arrange.

Besides checking your physical house, check your mental world. As you go through experiences, keep thinking of ways to explain them to your child on the proper level. She is constantly learning about the world and trying to figure it out, and you can help her by appropriate explanations. Moreover, sharing will be more fun for you than not. Parents are children's number one teachers. You know them better than anyone else and therefore are often the best ones for teaching and explaining. Think of how many hours you spend together and how much you can offer during those times.

Because of our fast-moving way of life, we spend hours and hours en route and then even more hours and hours waiting, in doctors' offices, restaurants, for buses, planes, or trains, etc. Try to figure out appealing games and projects that are easy to take with you for use at unexpected times. One idea is a 3″ × 5″ index card notebook. One per page, fill it with letters from A to Z, capital and lowercase, numbers, words, equations, or other symbols.

As your child flips through it, talk about what she sees. Do not ask "What is that letter, word, etc.?" Just play. She can also use the book to trace any of the writing in the book. An interesting pen (there are so many available now) and a small pad are wonderful. They give your child the opportunity to create. In addition, there are so many writing games you can share together. There are dots, tic-tac-toe, finish the pattern,

and any others you may know. Look around for large-print signs for reading and places like elevators for letter and number recognition. Count objects together and look for shapes both indoors and out. Remember about playing as you teach, and you both will be in for great rewards.

Helping around the House

Children should be introduced to as many jobs around the house as possible. They want to be helpful. It gives more meaning to their lives to participate than to have everything done for them. Try to find easy responsibilities at first and continue to add more as they grow. Sorting and folding clothes including matching socks is a good starter. Clearing dishes and later setting the table are appropriate. Any help in cooking like mixing, measuring, and pouring can be taught. Dusting and sweeping are also possible. A child should be shown where everything goes in her room and asked to be as responsible as possible for her belongings. Try to teach work in the house as positive fun. Bring out the satisfaction of doing a job well and taking care of oneself and one's things. If there are several areas that need attention, you can even make it into a game activity. Write each job on a separate index card, like "sweep the floor," "dust the furniture," "clean a mirror," "set the table" (with play dishes or real), "tidy a drawer," etc., and place the cards in a pile. Ask your child to pick a card and read it with your help to the best of her ability. Then work on the task together. Working and playing together makes your activities and hers much more meaningful.

Sometimes jobs at home are done more easily and efficiently by you alone. It does not mean that everything should be done together, but it does mean that many activities are worth a try.

A Few Words about Nutrition

Proper nutrition plays as important a role in the home environment of a child as her physical surroundings and activities. The key concept is a balanced diet. Just as a child needs a balanced program of active and quiet activities, creative and regimented ones, so she needs to eat from the four basic food groups—milk, meat, fruits and vegetables, and breads and cereals. The meals each day do not have to be perfectly balanced, but if you notice the same imbalance day after day, you can then change the diet. With an older child you can work together on the food chart presented in this chapter and help her understand how to eat in a balanced way.

The only exception to the above concept of balanced eating is the milk group. That group has come under recent scrutiny by doctors and nutritionists. There is some evidence that milk in its present homogenized form and all dairy products in their present processed form are difficult to digest for many people. Decreasing dairy products and eliminating sugars, white flour, and artificial colors and flavors has become an accepted way of treating hyperactivity, some childhood problems, and some learning disabilities. It is wise to check with a doctor or nutritionist before going on any special diet that deviates from a balance of the four food groups.

The food chart is to aid you in developing a proper diet for your child and can also be used for yourself. Make a check mark in a space each time food from a certain group is eaten on a particular day. Often foods do not clearly belong in one group, but you can fit them into the categories that are closest. A food like pizza provides a serving in more than one category and can be checked off in more than one. There are no ounces or serving sizes marked because that is not the way we eat. Just make a judgment whether you have served the equivalent of one or two servings of the food and check it off accordingly. A serving for a child is smaller than one for an

A Balanced Diet

Try It!

For CANDY, CAKE, and COOKIES, one serving is enough	Day	O.K.	Be Careful	Too Much

	Day	Too Little	About Right			Too Much
MILK						
yogurt						
custard						
pizza						
cheese						
cottage cheese						
ice cream						
MEAT						
egg						
peanut butter						
pizza						
fish						
chicken						
FRUITS and VEGETABLES						
grapes tomato						
apple juices						
orange raisins						
berries banana						
figs melons						
BREADS and CEREALS						
pasta waffles						
crackers pancakes						
bagels pizza						
rice popcorn						
muffins granola						

adult. In the example of pizza, two slices for a six year old would require two checks in the bread and cereals group, one in the fruits and vegetables group, and one in the milk group. The same two slices for a three year old would require four checks in the bread and cereals groups, two in the fruits and vegetables group, and two in the milk group. This sheet can also help you plan your evening meal. Once you see what breakfast, lunch, and snacks have provided, you can add food from any groups that are low. These weekly sheets can also be helpful to adults who should also follow the same rules for proper nutrition.

The following is a sample day's menu. You can see on page 147 a picture of the balance of the diet on that day for this particular six-year-old girl.

Breakfast
orange juice
scrambled egg
1 slice of toast

Snack
granola bar

Lunch
tuna fish sandwich
sliced pineapple
cranberry juice

Snack
dish of ice cream

Dinner
hamburger
broccoli with cheese sauce
baked potato
milk
strawberries

A Balanced Diet Try It!	For CANDY, CAKE, and COOKIES, one serving is enough	Day	O.K.	Be Careful	Too Much
		Monday	✓		

MILK yogurt custard pizza cheese cottage cheese ice cream	Day	Too Little		About Right				Too Much
	Monday	✓	✓	✓				

MEAT egg peanut butter pizza fish chicken	Monday	✓	✓	✓				

FRUITS and VEGETABLES grapes tomato apple juices orange raisins berries banana figs melons	Monday	✓	✓	✓	✓	✓	✓	

BREADS and CEREALS pasta waffles crackers pancakes bagels pizza rice popcorn muffins granola	Monday	✓	✓	✓	✓			

The Birthday Party

One of the major events that happens for a child each year is her birthday. It marks for you and her a year of growth. It also carries with it new responsibilities for her and the idea of being capable of new achievements. Because your child looks forward to her special day for a long time, you have the job of trying to plan appropriate activities that will make that day for her as meaningful as possible.

A birthday party is the most popular way in which to celebrate a child's birthday. The rule of thumb for children's parties is to invite one more child than the age that the child is. For example, if she is five, you invite six children. Very often you have other social obligations and cannot abide by this rule, but it seems to work well if you can manage it. While it is nice to have children's parties in restaurants, children's theaters, parks, and at other special event places, for a young child who is first learning what a party is, there is no place like home. The simple traditions are the ones you want to teach before you change and elaborate on them as you might do for an older child.

Here are some birthday party activities that are easy to prepare and that will be meaningful even for a young child. You can expand the concepts for an older child who can do a little more. They do not include competition, but they do focus on participation. They all go well with a good serving of ice cream and cake and a simple lunch if you desire. No candy is necessary for their pleasure. Raisins (sometimes carob or yogurt covered), pretzels, potato chips (light or no salt), interesting cheese cubes or thin strips, melon pieces or other fruit, and sometimes vegetables with a dip are all well-received snacks.

PARTY ACTIVITIES

1. *Stickers on a present.* You can wrap up a favor for each child, the same or similar kind for everyone, and place a different sticker on each package. One at a time, give each child a card with a sticker on it that matches a sticker on a present. The child must correctly match the card to the present. After everyone makes their matches, they can all open their presents and place their discarded wrapping in a central carton, bag, or pail.

2. *Pass the present.* This game is similar to the well-known "hot potato" game. Tell all the children to sit in a circle. As you play music they pass a present wrapped in many layers of gift wrap. When you stop the music, the child who has the present opens one layer of wrap. When you start the music, the children continue to pass it. You continue in this way until the present is completely unwrapped. The present should be something that has a piece for every player, like a group of children's rings, bracelets, notepads, etc.

3. *Color happy birthday.* Write out

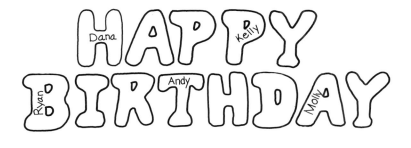

_ _ _ _ _ _ _ _ _ _ _ _ _ _ _ _ _
Child's Name

in large thick letters that can be colored in on a large paper table cloth. Write the name of each of the guests in one or more of the letters. They can then color the letters that are designated with their own names.

4. *Acting out children's records.* There are several records that children can enjoy by following along with actions. One is *Sesame Street Exercise* by the Children's Television Workshop. Another is *The Bean Bag Record* by Kimbo. There are others, but they are hard to find. Some specialty educational toy stores will let you listen to the records like these first before you buy them. If you have this opportunity, check to make sure the actions are easy enough to follow. Explain to the children before you play it what they are going to do. Another idea is to play a popular hit record for the children to dance.

5. *Activities with blocks and puzzles.* If you have a large quantity of any one kind of blocks, introduce them as a play activity. Judge by the age and size of your group what kinds and numbers of blocks would be appropriate. After they play freely for a while, ask them to build something specific like a train, tower, or castle. For puzzles give each child his own, if you have enough, or set them up as partners. You can set a timer and see who can complete their puzzle before the timer rings. You might want to do another round after switching the puzzles.

6. *The acting game.* There are lots of different categories of actions you can write out on a group of index cards, one action per card. You could use animals, careers, or action words or phrases. In turn, each child picks a card and acts out what it says. If the children are old enough, you could show the child her card secretly. Then as she acts it out, the other children try to guess what her card said. Here are some examples. You could make up many, many more.

Animals	*Careers*	*Actions*
Dog	Police Officer	Hop
Cat	Fire Fighter	Jump
Elephant	Teacher	Clap
Horse	Doctor	Sing
Cow	Secretary	Eat food
Pig	Bus Driver	Drive a car

7. *Talent show.* Ask each child in turn to sing a song, dance, or do some special gymnastics. Clap for each participant.
8. *Party favors.* A good party favor is a simple plastic beach ball. They usually cost well under a dollar. If weather and time permit, you could take the children outside with their beach balls, help them blow them up, and play with all of their balls at one time. Other good presents are interesting note pads, crayons, inexpensive puzzles and books, and one can of play dough from a carton of four.

From special days like birthdays to every day, there are many worthwhile, interesting, and enjoyable activities we can do with our children. I hope that the suggested activities in this book will provide you and your child with many happy hours of playing and learning together.

Bibliography

Ayers, A. Jean. *Sensory Integration and the Child.* Los Angeles: Weskin Psychological Services, 1979.

Doman, Glenn. *How to Teach Your Baby to Read.* Garden City: Doubleday and Co., 1975.

Goldberg, Sally. *Teaching with Toys.* Ann Arbor: University of Michigan Press, 1981.

Gregg, Elizabeth M. *What to Do When "There's Nothing to Do."* New York: Dell Publishing Co., 1968.

Kay, Evelyn. *Games That Teach for Children Three through Six.* Minneapolis: T. S. Denison and Co., 1981.

Lorton, Mary Baratta. *Workjobs: Activity-Centered Learning for Early Childhood Education.* Menlo Park, Calif.: Addison-Wesley Publishing Co., 1972.

Suzuki, Shinichi. *Nurtured by Love: The Classic Approach to Talent Education.* Smithtown, N.Y.: Exposition Press, 1982.

Game Cards

the 1	he 11	at 21	but 31	there 41
of 2	was 12	be 22	not 32	use 42
and 3	for 13	this 23	what 33	an 43
a 4	on 14	have 24	all 34	each 44
to 5	are 15	from 25	were 35	which 45
in 6	as 16	or 26	we 36	she 46
is 7	with 17	one 27	when 37	do 47
you 8	his 18	had 28	your 38	how 48
that 9	they 19	by 29	can 39	their 49
it 10	I 20	word 30	said 40	if 50

the 1	he 11	at 21	but 31	there 41
of 2	was 12	be 22	not 32	use 42
and 3	for 13	this 23	what 33	an 43
a 4	on 14	have 24	all 34	each 44
to 5	are 15	from 25	were 35	which 45
in 6	as 16	or 26	we 36	she 46
is 7	with 17	one 27	when 37	do 47
you 8	his 18	had 28	your 38	how 48
that 9	they 19	by 29	can 39	their 49
it 10	I 20	word 30	said 40	if 50

(Cut along the dotted lines)

159

will 51	some 61	two 71	my 81	long 91
up 52	her 62	more 72	than 82	down 92
other 53	would 63	write 73	first 83	day 93
about 54	make 64	go 74	water 84	did 94
out 55	like 65	see 75	been 85	get 95
many 56	him 66	number 76	call 86	came 96
then 57	into 67	no 77	who 87	made 97
them 58	time 68	way 78	oil 88	may 98
these 59	has 69	could 79	now 89	part 99
so 60	look 70	people 80	find 90	over 100

(Cut along the dotted lines)

161

will 51	some 61	two 71	my 81	long 91
up 52	her 62	more 72	than 82	down 92
other 53	would 63	write 73	first 83	day 93
about 54	make 64	go 74	water 84	did 94
out 55	like 65	see 75	been 85	get 95
many 56	him 66	number 76	call 86	came 96
then 57	into 67	no 77	who 87	made 97
them 58	time 68	way 78	oil 88	may 98
these 59	has 69	could 79	now 89	part 99
so 60	look 70	people 80	find 90	over 100

(Cut along the dotted lines)

Games for Reading Development

✂ (Cut along the dotted lines)

165

Word Cards

(p. 18)

Hop, Jump, and Clap

(p. 20)

Bookshelf Books

(p. 8)

Reading Book

(p. 13)

This Is a . . .

(p. 21)

Message

(p. 22)

Child's Magazine

(p. 14)

Categories Book

(p. 15)

Read

Read

Read

Read

Games for Writing Development

✂ (Cut along the dotted lines)

Copy and Color in Shapes

(p. 24)

Following a Maze

(p. 28)

Games for Reading Development

Letters

(p. 16)

Write

Write

Read

Read

170

Games for Writing Development

✂ (Cut along the dotted lines)

Crossing Out Letters

(p. 30)

Choosing Shapes
from a Group

(p. 30)

Picture Copying

(p. 25)

Fashion Plates
or Variation

(p. 26)

Write

Write

Write

Write

(Cut along the dotted lines)

Copy a Pattern

(p. 33)

Color by Number

(p. 32)

Follow the Dots

(p. 27)

Tracing

(p. 28)

Write

Write

Write

Write

Games for Writing Development

✂ (Cut along the dotted lines)

Writing on Lined Paper

(p. 36)

Letter Writing

(p. 37)

Chalkboard Writing

(p. 34)

"Show Me" Game

(p. 34)

Write

Write

Write

Write

(Cut along the dotted lines) ✂

Play and Say

(p. 40)

I See

(p. 41)

Word Memory

(p. 44)

Spell a Word

(p. 45)

Talk

Talk

Talk

Talk

Games for Language Development

✂ (Cut along the dotted lines)

179

Who, What, Where, When, Why

(p. 42)

Describe an Outfit

(p. 43)

Write a Word for Speech

(p. 47)

Yes Game

(p. 47)

Talk

Talk

Talk

Talk

Games for Language Development

 (Cut along the dotted lines)

Rhymes

(p. 44)

Games for Listening and Thinking Development

Hide the Timer
or the Music Box

(p. 50)

Stringing Beads in
the Order Directed

(p. 53)

? ? Talk Talk

Games for Listening and Thinking Development

(Cut along the dotted lines)

183

Tap a Pattern

(p. 50)

Memorizing

(p. 54)

Simon Says

(p. 51)

Story of the Day

(p. 54)

✂ (Cut along the dotted lines)

Games for Listening and Thinking Development

Carry Out Commands

(p. 52)

Call Time

(p. 52)

Story of the Body

(p. 55)

Story of the People

(p. 57)

Games for Listening and Thinking Development

✂ (Cut along the dotted lines)

187

I See . . . and Discuss

(p. 60)

The Time Center

(p. 61)

Choosing Objects
in a Room

(p. 58)

Choosing Objects
from a Group

(p. 58)

✂ (Cut along the dotted lines)

What's Missing?

(p. 59)

Association

(p. 63)

Visualization

(p. 60)

Planning

(p. 64)

Games for Midline Development

✂ (Cut along the dotted lines)

191

Midline Matching

(p. 66)

Checkerboard Patterns

(p. 66)

Arms Together
Side to Side

(p. 70)

Jack-in-the-box

(p. 71)

Games for Midline Development

✂ (Cut along the dotted lines)

Yarn over Head
and Across

(p. 67)

Roll a Small Ball

(p. 68)

Leg and Arm Balance

(p. 72)

Body Midline Strength

(p. 73)

(Cut along the dotted lines)

Row, Row, Row
Your Boat

(p. 73)

Pat-a-Cake

(p. 74)

Eye Exercise

(p. 69)

Cross the Midline

(p. 69)

 (Cut along the dotted lines)

Board Games

(p. 81)

Bingo

(p. 83)

Lotto

(p. 78)

Dominoes

(p. 78)

Go

Go

Go

Go

198

(Cut along the dotted lines)

Memory Game

(p. 80)

Dots

(p. 83)

Mr. Mighty Mind

(p. 80)

Cards

(p. 85)

Go

Go

Go

Go

Games for Mathematics Development

(Cut along the dotted lines)

Number Containers

(p. 94)

Money Containers

(p. 95)

Ten Little Indians

(p. 88)

Find the Number

(p. 89)

+ and −

+ and −

+ and −

+ and −

Games for Mathematics Development

✂ (Cut along the dotted lines)

Money on the Spot

(p. 96)

Math in a Flash

(p. 97)

The Counting Game

(p. 90)

Counting Backward

(p. 91)

+ and −

+ and −

+ and −

+ and −

Games for Mathematics Development

✂ (Cut along the dotted lines)

Puzzle Math

(p. 98)

The Little Professor

(p. 98)

Copying Equations

(p. 92)

Equations

(p. 93)

+ and −

+ and −

+ and −

+ and −

Games for Gross Motor Development

(Write your child's name on the back of each card.)

✂ (Cut along the dotted lines)

Sponge Ball through a Hole

(p. 108)

Bowling

(p. 108)

Bike Riding

(p. 102)

Roller-Skating

(p. 103)

Games for Gross Motor Development

(Write your child's name on the back of each card.)

✂ (Cut along the dotted lines)

Movement in Space

(p. 103)

Golf

(p. 109)

Exercises

(p. 104)

Tennis

(p. 110)

Games for Gross Motor Development

(Write your child's name on the back of each card.)

✂ (Cut along the dotted lines)

Using a Large Ball

(p. 106)

Hide-and-Seek

(p. 111)

Bat and Ball

(p. 107)

Games for Fine Motor Development — Manipulative

(Cut along the dotted lines)

Straw or Pencil Passing

(p. 120)

Twisting and Braiding

(p. 121)

Play Dough and Clay

(p. 114)

Sewing

(p. 115)

Games for Fine Motor Development — Manipulative

(Cut along the dotted lines)

Where Is Thumbkin?

(p. 116)

Wheels on the Bus

(p. 117)

Piano

(p. 121)

Spinner

(p. 122)

✂ (Cut along the dotted lines)

Making Doll Clothes
without Sewing

(p. 119)

Homemade Puzzles

(p. 119)

Building Toys

(p. 123,

Open Shut Them

(p. 123)

✂ (Cut along the dotted lines)

Pegboard Patterns

(p. 128)

Button Practice

(p. 129)

Tearing and Pasting
Paper

(p. 125)

Jacks and/or Buttons
Pickup

(p. 125)

½

½

½

½

Games for Fine Motor Development — Pincer

(Cut along the dotted lines)

Clothespin Puppets

(p. 126)

Typewriter

(p. 127)

Stringing Macaroni
or Cereal

(p. 130)

Itsy Bitsy Spider

(p. 130)

½

½

½

½

✂ (Cut along the dotted lines)

223

Windup Toys

(p. 133)

Lifting Weights

(p. 136)

Telephone

(p. 127)

Lacing a Shoe

(p. 131)

¼

¼

½

½

✂ (Cut along the dotted lines)

The Tossing Game

(p. 133)

Hammering

(p. 134)

Yo-yo

(p. 137)

Zip

(p. 138)

¼

¼

¼

¼

✂ (Cut along the dotted lines)

Pouring

(p. 135)

Potato Carry

(p. 136)

Spooning

(p. 138)

¼

¼

—

¼

¼